Alone
No Longer

Other books by Joseph M. Champlin:

DON'T YOU REALLY LOVE ME?
CHRIST PRESENT AND YET TO COME
TOGETHER FOR LIFE
TOGETHER IN PEACE
THE MASS IN A WORLD OF CHANGE
THE SACRAMENTS IN A WORLD OF CHANGE
PREPARING FOR THE NEW RITE OF PENANCE
THE LIVING PARISH
THE NEW YET OLD MASS

Alone No Longer

Joseph M. Champlin

Ave Maria Press / Notre Dame / IN 46556

Acknowledgment

Excerpts from the text of the New American Bible, copyright © 1970 by the Confraternity of Christian Doctrine, Washington, D.C., are used by permission of copyright owner. All rights reserved.

Nihil Obstat:

> Rev. John L. Roark
> Censor Deputatus

Imprimatur:

> Most Rev. Francis J. Harrison, D.D.
> Bishop of Syracuse

© 1977 by Ave Maria Press, Notre Dame, Indiana

Library of Congress Catalog Card Number: 77-77817
International Standard Book Number: 0-87793-134-8

Printed and bound in the United States of America.

Contents

Prologue: A New Me?

During the past eight years prior to my present appointment as the 1976-77 pastor-in-residence at the North American College in Rome, Italy, I had been working at a feverish pace, juggling many sometimes conflicting responsibilities with my own interior peace being one of them.

For three of those years I served in a staff position for the United States Bishops' Committee on the Liturgy. In addition to that office task, I lectured extensively around the country, authored a weekly news column as well as several books, and still labored in the parish ministry on weekends at a suburban Washington church.

On May 1, 1971, I left the nation's capital and returned to my home diocese, becoming pastor of Holy Family Church in Fulton, New York. My expectations then were for a simpler life, one withdrawn from the travel, writing and lecture cycle, with concentration on pastoral duties.

That was not to happen. The speaking requests did not cease, but escalated. There seemed both a public demand and my own inner need to write the weekly column and a few more books. Invitations to serve on important committees in the local community as well as on diocesan, statewide and national religious commissions were offered and accepted. Moreover, I felt most anxious about fulfilling conscientiously the duties of a pastor and rejected any inclination to become a part-time, never-present parish priest.

To balance all these activities and discharge those multiple obligations reasonably well required careful use of my time, relatively few days off, plus an often tight and hectic schedule.

Those were eight highly productive and I must say quite satisfying years. But during the last few a certain subtle loss of peace, an interior restlessness crept into my conscious and unconscious self. I began to recognize new inner tensions and contradictions. I was weary of another trip, but not content just to stay home. I grew tired of meetings and committees, yet felt pleased to be asked and anxious to serve upon them. I kept hoping for a period of quiet, but deep down became even a bit bored after several weeks of routine work and a less demanding schedule.

Around this time Marriage Encounter took our parish by storm. A few years earlier we had sponsored an information night for interested couples, but they—and I—did not respond. However, in June, 1975, we hosted a second explanation evening. At that session 10 of our couples signed up for specific weekends and made their deposits, even though they had serious reservations and hesitations about the movement.

Within several months all had returned from their weekends deeply moved, full of joy and highly enthusiastic. Marriage Encounter was on its way at Holy Family. Within a year over 50 couples in the parish and local community had made weekends.

I was greatly impressed by the results I saw in those couples and I felt a need to make my own weekend, if for no other reason than to share more intimately in what was now a rich, important part of their lives. They also badly wanted their pastor to experience Marriage Encounter.

However, I went on my initial weekend with much reluctance and many reservations, a few of which are described in this book. Nevertheless, I also looked forward to those 44 hours away from parish work as something of a retreat, a welcomed opportunity to step back from those eight years and evaluate myself.

As I walked into the Sheraton Motel for the Marriage Encounter weekend, I wondered if I would find or rediscover "a quiet stream underneath the fluctuating affirmations and rejections of my little world."[1] I hoped I would. I wanted to become more acutely aware of that "still point where my life is anchored and from which I can reach out with hope and courage and confidence."[2]

And I did discover that quiet stream. I did become aware of this still point inside of me. The weekend itself was profoundly moving, the deepest experience of my life since ordination 20 years earlier. However, unlike many retreats with their often painful return to reality the day afterwards, the impact of my Marriage Encounter intensified in the weeks and months which followed. I felt a difference within myself and many, but not all, around me noticed certain changes in my external attitudes and behavior.

Six months later I made what is called a deeper or team-training Marriage Encounter in the New York City area. It continued the original weekend's effect of opening me up to my spouse, the People of God.

This book does not attempt to present a technical

---

[1] Henri J. M. Nouwen, *The Genesee Diary: Report from a Trappist Monastery* (Doubleday & Company, Inc.: Garden City, New York), 1976, p. xii.
[2] *Ibid.*, p. xii.

explanation or detailed description of Marriage Encounter or of those two weekends. It does, however, give a very brief summary of both the initial and deeper session so the reader, unfamiliar with the movement and the weekends, may understand the background of my remarks. For a fuller published treatment, one of several available texts[1] might be consulted.

The book's major direction, however, is to simply give my own personal reactions to various aspects of Marriage Encounter as they have affected me in the past two years.

The motivation behind this decision to compile and publish these reactions is mixed. First of all, when I have been deeply moved by an experience there usually is an internal need to express it publicly; thus some reflections will surface in my writings, through a column, an article, or a book. Then too I hope it may interest and encourage couples to make a Marriage Encounter. For already-encountered persons, I trust the volume may bring positive memories and support them in their efforts to grow as couples. And then, realizing that many priests and other clergy share the curiosity and anxiety about Marriage Encounter which I experienced, I hope that my words will help not only to alleviate this anxiety but perhaps even dispose them to make their own weekends. Finally, I discovered in Marriage Encounter numerous valuable insights into and aids for an individual's spiritual life. These touched areas such as prayer, sacred scripture, self-discipline, love for others, fraternal correction, the understanding of God as our Father, the sacraments of matrimony and the priesthood, strengthening the family, and renewing and building up the Church.

---

[1] As a source for literature and information write to either or both of the following headquarters: National Marriage Encounter, 955 Lake Drive, St. Paul, MN 55120; Worldwide Marriage Encounter, 3711 Long Beach Blvd., Long Beach, CA 90807.

Through these pages of intimate sharing—an always risky and vulnerable style of writing, as well as an unusual type of book for me—perhaps readers who are concerned about their love for themselves, for God, and for others may reap benefits similar to those which I derived from my own Marriage Encounter experiences.

The incidents and people mentioned in this volume are all real, but names and minor details have been altered to avoid any possible embarrassment to them.

I would like to thank several persons who shared in typing this manuscript from my increasingly illegible handwriting: Jean Germano of Rome, Italy; Nancy Galizia, Patricia Reilly and Sandy Weston of Fulton, New York.

Needless to say, I am deeply indebted to those countless couples, especially the spouses involved in Marriage Encounter and one family in particular, whose great love for me made this book a possibility.

1

A Few Explanations

Marriage Encounter is essentially a 44-hour crash course in loving communication for a husband and wife who have a good marriage, but would like to make it an even better one.

This experience normally takes place on a weekend beginning Friday night and concluding late Sunday afternoon.

A Marriage Encounter is not for problem solving, although sometimes couples seriously affected by marital difficulties, but with a spark of love still flickering between them, find that the new awarenesses and approaches gained through the weekend may ease or resolve their troubles.

Neither is it a social weekend, group therapy or a sensitivity training session. Husband and wife concentrate on each other and are asked to speak little or not at all of their personal lives with the couples who join them for the weekend.

While evaluated and approved by psychologists, Marriage Encounter still is a rather intense experience which involves considerable introspection and normally stirs up the participants' emotions. For that reason, individuals with severe emotional or mental conflicts or anxieties should not be encouraged to make a weekend.

The original Marriage Encounter was a Roman Catholic development with some Catholic practices (e.g., an optional concluding Mass) and basic Catholic theological concepts (e.g., the sacraments of matrimony and priesthood). However, many couples, not Roman Catholics, have made and enjoyed weekends, and have not felt particularly uncomfortable in the Catholic atmosphere. Today several outgrowths of the original Marriage Encounter, e.g., Jewish and Protestant expressions, exist in the United States.

Celibate priests and religious can and do make Marriage Encounters. Their spouse is the Church, God's people whom they serve and love. Priests dialogue either alone with the Father, or with the priest leader, or with another priest or religious brother making the weekend.

The Basic Weekend

Sometimes called also the original or initial weekend for a couple, this Friday-to-Sunday experience is the essence of Marriage Encounter. Everything afterwards has been designed simply to reinforce the concepts and techniques taught during those 44 hours of the basic weekend.

Around 25 married couples gather at a motel, retreat house or similar location around 7:30 P.M. on Friday night. They are led through the Marriage Encounter by the "presenting team"—three couples and a priest.

The team members alternate in giving 15 talks, each one carefully written out beforehand, critiqued by other veteran Marriage Encounter personnel, then reworked to insure they are faithful to the weekend outline, highly personal, extremely human and rich in content.

After every presentation the participants, separately and alone, write in a notebook their responses to a question linked with the talk. Following the designated period for writing, the partners meet in their room and read each other's reactions. They learn and understand, as the weekend progresses, why Marriage Encounter terms these "love letters to my spouse."

The very personal nature of Marriage Encounter makes it frustrating, even impossible for encountered couples to explain adequately what takes place during those 44 hours. The interested, but hesitant person may find that inability or unwillingness to discuss the details of a Marriage Encounter irritating, as if the initiated were concealing something which should be revealed. Information Nights sponsored by Marriage Encounter do offer answers to questions pertaining to the externals of the weekend, but one can truly grasp the reality only by experiencing it.

The Team-training Weekend

Called also a deeper or second weekend, the team-training weekend has been designed to prepare couples and priests for service later as part of the seven-person team giving presentations.

The weekend actually begins a month or so earlier with a kickoff meeting between the couple or priest and some veteran Marriage Encounter team personnel. The candidates, as it were, are given about 80 mimeographed pages containing precis of the basic weekend talks and are requested to read them, then write responses to these questions:

"Why does the weekend include this particular talk?"

"Why does it occur in this part of the weekend?"

"What did it mean to me on the original weekend and what effect is it having on me now?"

The team-training weekends take place at motels, retreat houses or colleges in several centers throughout the United States, e.g., Boston, New York, Chicago, Dallas.

It follows the basic format and content of the original encounter, but with an even tighter discipline and extensive optional open sharing by the couples.

A priest and one couple give all the presentations which are shorter than on the initial weekend; they offer deeper insights into the related topics and incorporate testimonies of personal experiences by the lead individuals.

The weekend is broken into two-hour segments, each of which includes a presentation, optional open sharing by the participating couples for an hour or so on a question suggested to them by the leaders, writing love letters to one's partner for about 10 minutes in response to a question also indicated by the leaders and, finally, dialogue between the spouses. Those 120-minute blocks are repeated over and over on different subjects.

A sample sharing question, to illustrate: "What changes have you experienced in your relationship with each other since Marriage Encounter and how has that changed your relationship with God?"

The question for a love letter and dialogue which followed this particular discussion was: "What are my deepest feelings about our Father now?"

On my deeper weekend, there were 35 couples and six priests from all over the East Coast and Canada as well as my own partner, a priest I had never met who was on his way back to Ireland.

The voluntary sharing by these couples and priests overwhelmed me. I jotted down, for instance, in the margin of my notebook during the responses to the question above, "enormously moving." Later, to my partner I wrote:

"I feel drained by the absolutely magnificent series of testimonies, including your own about God and Marriage Encounter. It is just another proof that God certainly has to be present in a special way throughout the weekend and afterwards. I hope we can be good instruments in communicating this message to others."

At the weekend's conclusion, couples and priests are usually assigned to a team for a basic weekend and begin writing their own presentations in preparation.

Dialogue

Marriage Encounter seeks to teach married couples the technique of dialogue. That word frequently is used to denote a specialized method of communication commonly termed a "ten and ten" — 10 minutes for writing a love letter on a mutually agreeable question, 10 minutes for sharing those written responses.

The letters are not intellectual essays, but free-flowing, honest accounts of one's feelings about a certain subject. For example, "How do I feel about our move to another city?"

In the exchange after writing, the spouses try to capture or share as closely as possible the other's feelings. The more that is achieved, the deeper the joy experienced between husband and wife and the greater their oneness felt.

Priests may dialogue in a variety of ways: with another priest as a partner; with themselves, but by writing a letter to the Lord in response to God's message found, for example, in sacred scripture; or with a couple.

National and International

Father Gabriel Calvo, a young Spanish priest working with couples from Barcelona, developed in 1962 an experimental weekend program to help husbands and wives improve and deepen their marital relationships.

Called "the Encuentro Conyugal" it spread rapidly throughout Spain and later to other basically Spanish-speaking areas.

Leaders of the Christian Family Movement brought an English-language version to the United States in August, 1967. The next summer these "Marriage Encounter" weekends really took root and in the decade since nearly a half-million couples have made this 44-hour experience.

For various complex reasons, two very similar, yet quite different, forms of Marriage Encounter have developed in our country.

One, National Marriage Encounter, with an office currently in St. Paul, Minnesota, is less structured and more loosely organized. It strongly encourages the daily "ten and ten" dialogue described above, but views this as only one form of communication. Moreover, it has an ecumenical approach.

The other, Worldwide Marriage Encounter, presently with an office in Long Beach, California, is more structured and tightly organized. It gives heavier stress to dialogue both on the weekend and afterwards. Furthermore, it has a greater Roman Catholic orientation.

My experience and this book are based upon Worldwide Marriage Encounter, the form almost exclusively operative in our own and neighboring cities of the Syracuse diocese.

Monthly Renewal

After the original weekend couples are encouraged to make monthly renewals. Normally these three-hour evening sessions include a review presentation on some concept from Marriage Encounter, an opportunity for open sharing, a dialogue period for spouses on a given question, Mass, and a half hour or so of socializing.

My limited observation indicates that 25 to 50 percent of the couples continue with monthly renewals. I would also judge the percentage of those who dialogue daily as much less. However, in my experience at least, 90 to 95 percent return with positive reactions from the original weekend and see at least some change or growth in their marital relationship.

2

Timeless, Jobless, Friendless

I was in a terrible mood at the parish during the Friday afternoon just prior to the start of my initial Marriage Encounter weekend.

Leaving for a few days, especially over a weekend, means last-minute phone calls, quick desk clearing and the frantic arrangement of many items which you deem must be completed before departure is possible. That pressurized and uncomfortable rushing has been a common experience for me over the past eight years, as time and time again I have dashed to the airport for another trip and another speaking engagement.

But this Friday was different. I snapped at people over the phone and barked at those in the rectory, both rather unusual responses for me. Above all I felt an edginess, a sourness, an irritation inside.

It seems we often do not understand the reason behind such negative feelings until hours or days afterwards. Following the weekend, I judged those reactions originated in anxieties about the approaching Marriage Encounter.

There were, of course, unanswered questions. Despite a fairly clear picture of the weekend formed from reading and discussion with our encountered couples at Holy Family, I still appeared to be asking inside: How do I, a celibate priest, make a marriage encounter? Who will be my partner? Must I share my deepest inner feelings with a stranger? With other persons? Will I have to hug and kiss people hardly known to me? Most of us are uncomfortable facing the unknown, coping with a mystery or moving ahead when questions remain unanswered. I am no exception.

The nervousness and concealed irritability hardly subsided when I arrived at the motel and settled in for the opening conference. A torrential downpour left me soaked as I carried suitcase and a bag of goodies for the snack table (the latter, a suggestion made in the handwritten letter sent to me by one of the presenting couples a week earlier). I met only strangers, although some friendly and smiling ones tried to make us feel welcome and at ease. Finally, I sat in relative silence for a good hour as we waited until late arrivals appeared on the scene. My sense of being important and busy did not accept the delay very kindly, although I remained passive and outwardly uncomplaining.

Once the three presenting couples and the team priest began their remarks, however, a different attitude immediately descended on the group and over me. Our leaders said, "This is a working weekend." While they were gentle and gracious about the suggested directions, it became clear these people meant business.

No television. Take off your watches and leave them in the desk drawer. Don't call home ("We will inform you if there is an emergency"). Keep silence after each conference as you return to the room or stay in the conference area to write. Avoid asking personal questions of the other couples about their homes, families or jobs. Take notes. No going outside. A timeless, jobless, childless, friendless weekend they called it.

On my second or deeper or team-training weekend near New York City, the discipline was even stricter. The host couple, again gentle, but very businesslike, gave me clear rules to observe: "Your partner is Father so-and-so. You will be sharing the same room and should sit, eat and walk together. In that way, the couples will not feel sorry, if they see you alone and wish to reach out with a welcoming hand. We want them instead to concentrate on each other."

That last sentence sums up the reason for all this discipline and the strong insistence on silence throughout so much of the weekend. Marriage Encounter has been designed to deepen the relationship between a husband and wife, to draw them closer together, to help them achieve the "two in one flesh" union God holds out as an ideal for married couples. It also seeks to intensify a priest's closeness in love to his spouse, the Church, the people of God he serves.

The weekend has not been constructed to foster relationships among the many couples participating or to facilitate communication between them. Neither is it to provide a priest with an opportunity to meet, talk and relate better with married persons. As we will see later in this book, that in fact does happen to an amazing and joyful degree. But it develops only because the deeper love a husband and wife discover within themselves just spills out or overflows to others.

By putting aside watches, turning off the television and leaving behind children, friends and job, the married couple and priest participant become free, able to center attention on relationships. I can thus better concentrate on myself, on my spouse, on my God and, then, on the world of other people in my life.

I was truly impressed on both weekends and surprised during the first one by the couples' ready acceptance of this call to follow such a tightly disciplined regimen. When I watched these lay persons, presumably not accustomed to observing the retreat-like silence, walk quickly without a word back to their motel rooms or begin immediately to write without any verbal comment in the conference area, my wonderment increased. In similar fashion, they responded to the priest leader's frequent remarks about the "work" aspect of our weekend with only good-natured grumbling. That tough schedule meant, for example, constant effort from early Saturday morning to late that night with a respite only for meals and a 10-minute break afterwards. Push, push, push, it was, for 44 hours.

The childless, jobless, friendless element has a secondary effect, perhaps not fully envisioned by the Marriage Encounter founders. After my initial weekend, reflection and discussion with other encountered people led me to understand how this deemphasis of accidental attributes helps us to stress or discover instead the essential uniqueness of others.

In today's world we tend to be impressed or judge people by how they look, where they work and what they wear. The size of their family, the quality of their home, the cut of their clothes lead us to make judgments about them as persons. What you do, not who you are, counts.

Since we value productivity and success so much in modern society, simply *being* takes a back seat to *doing*. When illness, unemployment, retirement or old age seriously diminishes our ability to produce or do things, there enters within us a subtle feeling that we have less worth and are less valuable, less lovable, less precious in the eyes of others.

The weekend experience of relating or speaking at table to others, generally strangers, without reference to home, family or occupation proved awkward at first. Looking back, I found it difficult and cumbersome for the entire three days. This should not have surprised me since our normal conversations regularly never go beneath that level.

Psychiatrist Karl Menninger in his book, *Whatever Became of Sin?* maintains that stereotyping people is one of the current age's vices. We quickly categorize persons and put them in slots. Dr. Menninger admits that physicians and psychologists are equally guilty of this.

How easily we can write off an individual by saying or thinking, "He has problems." "She needs help." Similarly we make positive or negative judgments so often based on external appearances. The presence or absence of such qualities as wealth, power, education, beauty and personality frequently makes us accept or reject, like or dislike people. We never get beyond the surface and fail to recognize or look for an inner richness present in the individual.

The Marriage Encounter experience does not instantly correct that trend or turn all weekend graduates into living saints who always treat others with a delicate respect for their fundamental dignity and uniqueness as persons. But it does heighten one's awareness in this regard and points out the goal to be pursued.

An example might help here.

One of our encountered husbands holds a top executive position with a large corporation which operates a plant in Fulton. He was walking outside the building some months ago when a large tractor trailer pulled in to deliver cargo for the factory. The driver stopped, honked the air horn, waved, rolled down the window and shouted an enthusiastic greeting.

Several other executives and a few nonsalaried workers observed the exchange, then looked puzzled by this obvious friendly relationship between the white-collared employee and the T-shirted truck driver.

These mystified bystanders discovered the explanation in Marriage Encounter. Since both executive and truck driver had made weekends and participated in follow-up monthly renewal evenings, they felt a certain common bond. Moreover, the thrust of those 44 hours seemed to have dissolved the barriers which differing positions, education and income sometimes erect between persons in the 20th century.

3
Down on Myself

You can share a bit more personally in this chapter by stopping now for no more than a five-minute pause and completing the experiment which follows.

Take a piece of paper, plain on both sides.

On the front side, list during the next 60 seconds your virtues or good qualities.

Next, reverse the paper and this time spend 60 seconds writing down your vices, faults or bad qualities.

Finally, compare both lists. Which is longer? Which has the greater number of items?

For most people the "bad" side contains more items than the "good" side.

We have a strange, yet strong tendency to accentuate our failings and minimize our achievements.

For example. In listing a virtue, you probably insisted, consciously or unconsciously, that this good attribute be present always in your life. On the contrary, if a bad characteristic has appeared only once in your life span, then you quite likely felt inclined, even obligated to note that as a vice.

Several illustrations may help.

A mother with many children may be the model of patience and self-discipline for six days. However, if on the seventh morning she loses her temper and reacts severely to the youngsters, then this woman probably would judge herself an impatient mother; she likely would feel bad about the lack of self-control and be down on herself.

An alcoholic who has been faithful to a pledge of abstinence for five years, but on one evening through a variety of circumstances overindulges, would, once sobriety has been regained, normally experience deep guilt feelings. Moreover, that person in most cases would need to wage an intense struggle alone and with the help of friends against this painful sense of failure. The five years of progress is immediately forgotten, canceled out by the single evening's lapse.

An idealistic seminarian who stumbles once during a summer vacation may come down hard on himself and in this spirit of dejection judge that he is a bad person, an unfit candidate for the lofty goal of priesthood.

A priest, religious sister or brother, faithful and exemplary for many years, who falls from grace in a moment of surprise or weakness will undoubtedly ignore that long period of fidelity and dwell only on the regrettable failure.

The list, of course, can go on endlessly and each of us could with some reflection add our own personal instances.

My point here is not to condone the mistakes, deny the existence of sin, or ignore the value of healthy guilt feelings. Instead, we simply wish to note how we often exaggerate our vices and minimize our virtues, concentrate on the failure and overlook the successes.

That pattern tends to create within us a poor self-image. Deep down, very deep down and in a subtle, often hidden way, we are inclined to be uncomfortable with ourselves as persons. We judge that we are not really good, not of much intrinsic worth, and not therefore lovable in the sight of others.

In the musical, *Man of La Mancha,* Aldonza epitomizes the individual who, crushed by the past and the present, lacks any sense of self-worth. A prostitute and apparently the daughter of one, this woman finds herself loved by the noble visionary, Don Quixote. He calls her "Dulcinea" and asks Aldonza to be "his lady." Overwhelmed by this incredible gentleness and love, and confused by it, she strikes out strangely in anger at the Lord of La Mancha who truly cares for her. The song, "Aldonza," is this woman's description of herself, of her self-image. To her unusual lover she cries:

> "So don't reach out to me when your sweet 'Dulcinea' you call—I am only Aldonza. . . I'm no one, I'm nothing at all."[1]

"I'm no one, I'm nothing at all." Aldonza's self-image is one of self-hate, rather than self-love.

During my original weekend I watched tears flow down the cheeks of a woman in her late 20's or early 30's as she listened to Aldonza's song. My heart genuinely went out to this woman in her pain, but the concept of a low self-image had not yet hit home to me. The compassion for her was, I judge now, somewhat condescending. "Poor girl," I thought, "she probably has made some mistakes, or had a tough upbringing, or is struggling with personal problems."

But me identify with Aldonza? The concept of being down on myself or possessing a low self-image hadn't

---

[1] From *Man of La Mancha.*

yet hit home and didn't seem to have much relevance for me during the greater part of the basic weekend.

Still, a few uneasy feelings and unanswered questions raised their ugly heads.

Why do I find it difficult to show my very personal feelings, like tears?

Why am I so overconcerned about pleasing everyone?

Why does it bother me so badly, if one person doesn't like my homily, lecture or leadership?

Why do I need instant reassurance after a presentation or a sermon?

Why do I feel the need always to be number one and grow uncomfortable when merely an equal part of the team?

Why do I grow silent when I am hurt or disagreed with, but then discuss the injury or objection with people other than the one person directly involved?

Why must I always be the giver and grow uncomfortable when I am the receiver?

Why do I sometimes feel sad when I sense people seem to respect me, but can't get close to me?

Why must I be in charge or in control of myself at every moment, afraid to let go or let down?

In the weeks and months following the original Marriage Encounter, I came to an awareness that, despite my successes, my self-image was lower than I thought. The feelings of self-assurance, self-confidence, self-success tended to be based on what I could do or had done, not what I was or am. Consequently, it was very important for me to be successful, the leader, popular, busy, thought of highly by others. Similarly, I thus found it awkward to be dependent, vulnerable, totally open and receptive to the love of others.

"God does not make junk" is a strongly emphasized Marriage Encounter principle. The statement itself never has exerted a powerful impact upon me, but the truth behind these words gradually seems to be taking root in my being. The concept of self-image is both profound and elusive; one does not grasp it like a mathematical equation. Consequently, we need to ponder the issue regularly and slowly deepen our appreciation of the goodness God has placed within us.

"God does not make junk" is a contemporary expression of this fundamental text from Genesis (1:27, 31):

> God created man in his image; in the divine image he created him; male and female he created them. God looked at everything he had made, and he found it very good.

A limited involvement in Marriage Encounter has led me to believe that the root answer to all those unanswered questions above rests in my failure to accept deeply in the heart (my head already understands it) this goodness of God's creation. In a word, by not truly believing I am good, by ignoring or underplaying the goodness present, I find it difficult to see how others can see the good in me and love me. Aldonza experienced similar feelings when confronted with Don Quixote's love.

This is a serious oversimplification of a complex, subtle, intimately personal issue. But even a beginning awareness of our God-given specialness can prove enormously freeing.

At my team-training weekend I heard a wife summarize this entire chapter in one incident which occurred on her original Marriage Encounter. She commented in words directed to her husband:

On that Sunday morning I wrote a long love letter to you and in it expressed feelings about events we had never discussed. In fact I wrote down things I had never revealed to anyone else, ever. When I heard your steps outside the door, my heart leapt with excitement. Here, I thought, perhaps for the first time we were going to share feelings never before experienced between us. I was trusting you with all these difficult areas of my life.

But when I read the letter in which you just poured out the tremendous love you have for me, that all changed. Then I realized instead I just had to cast aside all these bad thoughts about myself, peel away those layers of poor feelings I have and discover the goodness which you see in me, the goodness which makes you love me so much.

4

Love: A Feeling or a Decision?

A young student for the priesthood had recently been introduced to an experienced Marriage Encounter couple in Texas. The handsome husband and extremely attractive wife invited this seminarian to their home for an evening of dinner and conversation.

After the meal, as they sat around talking, the guest became rather preoccupied, appeared troubled or worried. The couple lightly probed for an explanation, but received no satisfactory response.

The husband then astutely and accurately diagnosed the situation. In a very gentle way he asked the future priest:

"Do you feel attracted to my wife?"

The seminarian blushed, looked at the floor, shifted around in his place, moved to the edge of the chair, wrung his hands and uttered a barely audible, quite incomprehensible reply.

Confident he had touched on the key issue, the husband reassured the embarrassed visitor:

"Hey, that's OK. Stop worrying. Relax. Those are very natural, normal feelings. They are neither right nor wrong. They just are."

With these words, the young man looked up, pondered briefly the impact of what he had heard, then breathed a sigh of relief and collapsed back into the easy chair.

The frown on his forehead disappeared, tight muscles let go, and he felt that exhausted peace or serenity we experience when in a crisis situation a potential disaster has been avoided (the opponent's field goal attempt missed; the tumorous growth was benign; the answer is "yes").

Feelings have no morality. By themselves neither right nor wrong, they just are. What we do with them and how they influence our thoughts, words, actions or omissions is a different matter. But first we should simply accept them, "feel the feelings" as it were, not try to repress or repel them.

That crucial Marriage Encounter concept has enormous power for freeing humans from unfounded guilt and negative thoughts about themselves.

The seminarian's severe uptightness and his consequent liberation is by no means an exceptional illustration.

Priests, religious and single lay persons seeking to live as chaste celibates for religious motives struggle with similar inner conflicts. Those of us who were trained prior to the past decade often heard or read about saints who seemed more angelic than human. These accounts frequently conveyed the impression that those holy individuals never had a sexual thought or feeling from the age of three. That absence was likewise attributed to their single-hearted and complete dedication to God.

The example of such total generosity and purity of heart is inspiring, needed and helpful. However, the alleged connection between that and the reputed elimination of sexual feelings has unnecessarily heaped heavy burdens on many well-intentioned Christian pilgrims. The

mere presence of a thought or feeling concerning sex
thus means I have somehow failed in my commitment to
the Lord or to chastity. Their very existence in me says
I am already a failure and impure. My innocence with
regard to the origin of these feelings and the proper way
in which I handle those inner stirrings once present tend,
consequently, to be insignificant or irrelevant.

This attitude about feelings reaches out to other
areas besides sexuality.

I remember well visiting with a distressed daughter
in her 50's trying to cope with resentful feelings about an
80-year-old invalid mother. For a dozen years this woman
had led a heroic, confined life at home caring for that
demanding elderly lady. She and her husband had sacri-
ficed many trips and pleasures to spend time or give
services for the mother.

Creeping senility now was making the older lady
unreasonable, abusive and impossible to deal with phys-
ically or emotionally at the house. The only alternative
seemed a nursing home with professional medical personnel. The mother nevertheless bitterly attacked her
daughter for this move.

The daughter, exhausted by those extended efforts,
experienced real resentment over the "lost" period of
her life, the ingratitude, and the unreasonable accu-
sations. Despite the fact that she remained patient, loyal
and continued her tender care through frequent visits,
the woman judged herself severely guilty for merely having such resentful feelings. Again, she failed to grasp
the pure naturalness of feelings and their nonmorality.

Dying persons and those whose loved ones are
near death often experience feelings of anger and sadness. The anger may be directed to God for this cruel
fate; the sadness arises because of the impending loss
or separation.

A husband, for example, may inwardly feel like

angrily crying out: "Why, God? Why me? Why my wife? We have always been good Catholics and churchgoers; why not someone else?" Almost immediately guilt floods his being and deeply criticizes him for even feeling that way.

So, too, the fatally ill patient may experience a numbing sadness or depression, feelings most natural. To comfort the person, as we normally might, by whispering "Don't feel sad," almost complicates the situation. Better to show silently by a touch or in words that we recognize their sadness, accept it and are standing by their side through the ordeal.

The picture sometimes painted of Jesus so stresses his divinity, his power and strength, that we forget those many human feelings he manifested in the Gospels.

He wept over his dead friend Lazarus and, as a result, onlookers commented about the depth of his love for the man. He felt compassion for the widow whose only son was being buried. He showed anger in the temple and toward the Pharisees. He experienced a sad frustration over the inhabitants of Jerusalem and their unwillingness to accept his teachings.

Since Christ was like us in all things (including feelings) except sin, then our feelings in themselves cannot be sinful.

How does love fit in here? Isn't it also a feeling?

Love songs do speak normally in very emotional, feeling terms.

Movies, television plots and novels often equate love with some instant feeling or attraction for a person that leads swiftly to bed and sometimes to marriage.

The first falling in love experience of an adolescent usually manifests itself in multiple emotional ways. The boy feels good in her presence, carries the girl's books, loses interest in other things and people, speaks with his beloved for hours on the telephone. The girl has similar feelings and acts in parallel fashion.

More mature courtship tends to be steadier and less heady in emotion, but even so couples frequently evaluate the depth of their love by the intensity of their feelings.

The first romantic stage of marriage—one team couple called it the fun and rainbows period—we likewise associate with positive, pleasant feelings.

However, there are problems if we identify love with feelings. For instance, that initial love event inclines to be beautiful, high-powered, blind, compulsive, divorced from reality and temporary. Sooner or later, generally sooner, the young persons drift back to earth and those warm feelings disappear.

So, too, in time the glow and enthusiasm of a wedded couple may diminish, even in some matters disappear entirely, often bringing on a stage of disillusionment and serious questions about the love present in their relationship.

Moreover, if love is merely a pleasurable sensation, an enjoyable emotion, a positive feeling, why do we designate some difficult, painful, even death-bringing actions deeds of love? Mother Teresa picking up the "poorest of the poor" in Calcutta, a wife holding her vomiting child's forehead, a husband working two jobs, a priest spending two hours in the middle of the night by a hospital bed, Jesus on the cross—we would discover little or no pleasure there.

Love admittedly is a many-splendored thing. Pleasurable feelings often are connected with it. But Eric Fromm, in his *The Art of Loving,* seems nearer the truth when he maintains that love in essence is giving, selfgiving. That squares clearly with Christ's words about "greater love than this no person has than to lay down one's life for another" (Jn 15:13).

Marriage Encounter phrases the same principle in this way: Love is a decision. It is an act of the will and the intellect. Love means deciding to do or not do something in spite of our feelings and carrying out that decision in practice. We may feel like doing this or we may not. But our mind and heart tell us what should be done and our will carries it out.

Our Lord offers us a perfect example of these points in the Garden of Gethsemani. On that Holy Thursday night he felt deep sadness, causing him to exude a bloody sweat. The prospects of suffering and ultimate death stirred natural revulsion within him. Under so great a burden, he sought support from sleeping apostles and prayed to his Father for release from such a destiny.

However, when it became clear that Good Friday was the plan of God for him, Jesus made the loving decision to accept this fate and then willed to set forth on his mission.

The difficulty frequently for us rests in our failure to make those love decisions and carry them out in the face of conflicting feelings. Unlike Christ we do not always say "Yes, Father." Often the inner response is "No" or "I can't" or "I will try" or a halfhearted "Maybe."

Thus, lonely persons may feel their loneliness so intensely they reach out for something or someone to ease the painful feeling, knowing deep down it is not a love decision and will but further complicate matters.

Or the hurt, resentful, neglected spouse gets even in one way or another.

Or hungry restless individuals grab for what they know, despite its attractiveness, will sour and spoil their lives.

My 20 years of priestly experience has led me to believe that much, perhaps most human misery comes from our inability to understand, accept, cope with or direct feelings. We allow feelings to run our lives. We don't direct them; they direct us. The love decisions are too weak, not sufficiently strong in the face of contrary feelings.

St. Paul, in a classic passage, clearly describes the kind of struggle or tension which so often exists within us.

> I cannot even understand my own actions. I do not do what I want to do but what I hate. When I act against my own will, by that very fact I agree that the law is good. This indicates it is not I who do it but sin which resides in me. I know that no good dwells in me, that is, in my flesh; the desire to do right is there but not the power. What happens is that I do, not the good I will to do, but the evil I do not intend. But if I do what is against my will, it is not I who do it, but sin which dwells in me.
>
> This means that even though I want to do what is right, a law that leads to wrongdoing is always ready at hand. My inner self agrees with the law of God, but I see in my body's members another law at war with the law of my mind; this makes me the prisoner of the law of sin in my members. What a wretched man I am! Who can free me from this body under the power of death? All praise to God, through Jesus Christ our Lord! So with my mind I serve the law of God but with my flesh the law of sin (Rom 7:15-25).

Feelings are neither right nor wrong; they just are. These emotions ordinarily arise spontaneously as a result of some person, event or situation. Love, in regard to feelings, can mean a number of things: 1) a decision to accept our feelings just as they are, 2) a decision to avoid bringing on situations known to cause dangerous feelings for us, and 3) a decision to do the right thing or omit the wrong action despite our feelings.

An example to clarify this:

I have had great difficulty in coping with feelings of ambition during my priesthood. After all, a man of God should be humble, seek the last place, avoid glory and praise. But despite prayer and self-discipline those emotions and inner thoughts continued.

Since my image before others as a perfect priest was very important, I could not admit these feelings, especially to my peers in the ministry. As a result I would feel, deep down, rather ashamed of such emotions. How unworthy to even have those thoughts and desires! I didn't really trust any friend enough to share the anxieties for fear my image would be shattered and that individual put me down.

Only after Marriage Encounter and its treatment of love and feelings was that knot untied. Strange, too, that I first shared this with a mature, loving couple in whom I had great trust, rather than with a brother priest.

Together we came to see those were merely feelings, neither right nor wrong, over which I had no control. What a freeing experience, like that involving the Texas seminarian.

Love for me in this instance means simply to accept those emotions (often such an acceptance actually causes feelings to dissipate or subside).

Love, however, also includes a decision not to daydream excessively or build magic castles in the air, activities which merely bring on or intensify such ambitious thoughts.

Finally, love also, in this case, would exclude any type of manipulative action designed to achieve inappropriately those cherished goals or ambitions.

5
Married or Single: Alone or Together

This chapter speaks about pain, disillusionment and loneliness, as well as joy. It looks at married couples who live together, but are in reality sometimes quite alone. The section also discusses priests who work constantly among people, but still sometimes shut themselves off in isolation from them.

I have from my youngest days loved sports both as a participant and as a spectator. I played soccer, basketball and baseball at school, then in postcollege years I took up and continue today with handball, tennis and paddleball.

My spectator approach, nevertheless, assumes almost as active a stance as if I were one of the players involved. I watch intensely, shout with exultation or disgust over some key incident, identify with a team or player, and feel joy or sadness after the contest.

While as a young priest preparing and teaching a course to high school students, I suddenly discovered the reason behind my extreme engagement in sports as a spectator. In presenting the psychological differences between men and women, the textbook for my sessions stressed that men are more competitive than women, need to feel superior and frequently fulfill these needs by conquering through others. Thus in sports they are inclined to become one with their team or adopted players and win or lose through them.

That was me right on the button. I never watched games with a detached, objective attitude. The Redskins, Phillies, Knicks and Rangers were *my* teams and *I* was the conqueror or the vanquished with them.

In those romantic, early years after ordination, that fascination with sports did not prove a serious obstacle to my priestly work. My whole being was so filled with enthusiasm about the ministry that I had to push myself just to take a day off away from the parish. There were worlds to be conquered, souls to be saved, people in want of me. Each moment seemed to open up a fresh field ripe for the harvest or a new experience to stir my imagination. Interest in and need for sports was minimal.

But slowly and gradually—I can't remember when and hardly how—that fun and rainbows, hearts and flowers, romance stage of the priesthood at times disappeared.

Rituals so rich in the beginning became, on occasion, routine rites. Tasks previously filled with excitement often assumed the character of a dry obligation. People who once seemed totally loving and supportive now and then criticized or rejected my efforts. As an immature idealist I became disillusioned, experiencing the humanness of Church leaders and suffering through my own failures in the Christian life.

Still, there were those moments of joy which sustained me, particularly in the confessional, the rectory office and by the hospital bed. I felt needed and loved, tasted great satisfaction when able to heal and help wounded, hurting persons.

Nevertheless, moments of disillusionment were and can be trying. One is tempted during them to reach out in escape or pull back in isolation.

One of those escaping, isolating avenues for me would be an overemphasis on sports, particularly the spectator kind. This included that exaggerated, vicarious involvement with athletics via television and the printed media.

I am not saying here that for me or for others watching athletic contests in person or over television is bad, evil and morally wrong. Nor do I maintain that a close identification with a player or a team should be avoided. My point merely revolves around a lack of proportion or perspective, an undue emphasis on something basically recreational or diversionary.

In a subtle, small, but potent way, that involvement in spectator sports tended to pull me away from others. Despite the fact that I had accepted serving people as my purpose in priesthood, there was a growing desire on occasions to be totally undisturbed, free from them and by myself. Consequently, I resented intrusions during those private, isolated moments.

Unexpected callers at the rectory on a fall Sunday afternoon often received distracted attention and a swift answer to their requests (the two-minute warning in the football game had just been given). Telephoners might hear a baseball crowd in the background and sense my mind was only partially with their conversation. Colleagues wishing to visit about other matters during a televised contest usually gave up after 10 to 15 minutes and either joined in watching or went about another task. The housekeeper learned that normally during my breakfast reading of the sports page it was best not to pose questions or make conversation.

Again, I am not speaking about legitimate privacy, solitude and recreation needs for myself or other priests. Rather, it is the excessive or exaggerated characteristic which forms the point at issue.

That pulling away from others, typified by the sports example, yet exemplified in many parallel areas, unfortunately does not ease the pains of disillusionment. On the contrary, there frequently follows a certain amount of guilt, a greater sense of loneliness, a sad regret and then deeper disillusionment. It becomes almost a vicious circle.

Married couples experience similar romantic, disillusionment, and joyful stages in their relationships. The television set and spectator sports likewise often are escape avenues for one or both partners to become "single" again, even though still living together.

We have a rose garden beside our church at Holy Family clearly visible from the sacristy window. Just prior to the wedding ceremony I like to point out those bushes to the nervous groom. Later, in the homily, it gives me a visual example with which to discuss married life.

The buds possess a beauty delightful to behold and a fragrance pleasant to smell. But along the stem are sharp briars.

Marriage, too, has its buds and briars. For better, for worse, richer, poorer, sickness, health, in good times and in bad, bride and groom promise to love and cherish each other all the days of their lives.

I often wonder if the young man and woman really hear those comments.

Everything is beautiful in the beginning. Constant new discoveries, little surprises, excitement.

But in time the glow goes, the bubble bursts, the dream dissolves. He leaves underwear on the floor; she is never on time. He comes home late without calling; she seldom has dinner ready. His wife is not what he expected; he, too, is not the person she thought. Both become disappointed in themselves and rather disillusioned, at least in part, with their marriage. Neither they nor their nuptial union is as special as they thought.

True, they taste joy at times and feel moments of closeness. The birth of a baby and the serenity after making up, for example, show how much they care for each other and from time to time they do experience a sense of oneness. But more often the spouses seem to go their separate ways.

Our modern world does not help much here. Marriage Encounter maintains that the world's plan today is for husband and wife to live as "married singles." Don't be involved with each other. Live a separate kind of existence. Follow stereotype roles. Thus,

Husband: be the breadwinner; don't share work problems at home; keep your feelings inside; watch television by yourself after supper; let her do the dishes and care for the children.

Wife: the home is where you belong; remember he needs to be superior; keep the children and their affection for yourself; you are the heart, he is the head of the marriage.

I heard a husband and father of four describe with pained regret after his Marriage Encounter just how the television set had made him a "married single." The weekend experience led this extremely conscientious man to realize those hours parked in front of the color TV had truly isolated him from his wife and children. Granted he was in the house and not out with the guys or at a local bar, but still his presence was passive, unresponsive. In a way, he reigned as an aloof king, a stranger to spouse and offspring. He resented intrusions, objected to disturbing noises and generally didn't respond to the others' questions or indirect pleas for loving attention.

His pattern changed after Marriage Encounter. Having rediscovered a deeper love relationship with his wife and discovered the joy in a closer relationship with his children, he simply lost much of his previous interest in television. Gone, also, were some of the lonely feelings, the sad isolation, the disillusionment which accompanied those lengthy television hours.

I know at times he still watches his set and probably slips back sporatically into the former habits of a "married single." But such incidents are less often and less extensive. Moreover, he is aware now of a better goal, of being together with wife and children, not apart from them.

On my deeper weekend I heard a wife say to her husband: "You get up at 6:00 and go to work and I don't get up until 9:00. But then you are tired by 11:00 that night and want to get to bed. I am not tired, so I watch television. But I feel lonely and separated from you. From now on I am going to get up early with you, so I too will be tired when you are. I no longer want to be a married single."

The priest who presented my original weekend mentioned his own excessive addiction to television during a disillusionment period of his priesthood. Following Marriage Encounter, he found there was an automatic diminution in the number of hours spent before a set.

That reduction was not so much a conscious decision to avoid or reduce something bad or destructive. Instead, the shift in life pattern came from a reawakening and a deeper awareness of joys found in the relationship with his spouse, the Church, the people of God he serves.

A year is not a sufficently long testing period, but during the 12 months since my own Marriage Encounter I have seen a parallel personal modification. I watch television less, find my interest and involvement in spectator sports still present, but not so intense, discover that relationships with parishioners absorb more of my interest. Moreover, I certainly possess a deeper consciousness of what it means both to be a priest isolated from his people and married to them.

6

Somebody Loves Me

A priest friend, also a writer, mentioned some months back a novel called *Looking for Mr. Goodbar* which he felt successfully illustrated some contemporary problems.

I forgot about his suggestion until a week ago at JFK Airport in New York. While waiting for a flight to Rome, I saw the paperback on display at the newsstand. Remembering his recommendation, I bought a copy for the flight.

The first 150 pages seemed a waste of time and energy. The main character was Theresa Dunn, the standard mixed-up single girl living in New York. The book was typically heavy on sex with a few drug adventures sprinkled throughout the story. The plot was not particularly engaging. I started to put the book aside when lawyer James Morrisey entered the woman's life. A Fordham graduate in his late 20's or early 30's, he was quite intelligent, appeared shy but self-confident, timid but persistent.

Unlike Theresa's many other male acquaintances, he neither met her in a bar nor ended up in bed with the woman for a one-night stand. The lawyer simply liked her and had begun to care about her as a person.

On their first date, a dinner at Luchow's, Theresa acted with incredible crudeness despite the fact that she was a teacher, obviously intelligent and from a somewhat cultured family. With remarkable patience, he continued the conversation until she responded by opening up to him about her genuine dedication to teaching and her love for her students. This sort of self-exposure on Theresa's part was both attractive and surprising, and it resurrected my interest in the novel. Here was a modern-day Aldonza with James Morrisey playing Don Quixote. Would his ability to see and value her as a person be able to convince Theresa of her innate self-worth? Would she even accept it? Since no one had loved her like this before, I felt myself excited by the prospect of a change in this woman now that someone had offered her a fully human relationship.

Theresa was a true Aldonza. Her reactions to his tenderness and love were confusion, indifference, hostility. Despite all these inner conflicts, Theresa continued to see James, but acted out her confusion in occasional bursts of sarcasm. The relationship followed a pattern of gentle, patient, almost tenacious love on the part of Morrisey with erratic responses from Theresa. She liked him, but felt no deep sexual attraction for the man. Nevertheless, he was clearly getting close to her, even changing her way of looking at herself. As Theresa saw it,

> The real problem was that since she'd known James the act of picking up a man . . . wasn't simple any more; a whole dialogue had been set up in her mind in which he argued against it and she argued for it and when she won it didn't matter, because enough of his view lingered in her mind to take the edge off any possible pleasure . . . He had made her uncomfortable with her old life.[1]

---

[1] Rossner, Judith. *Looking for Mr. Goodbar.* New York: Pocket Books 1976, p. 270.

James was clearly in love with Theresa. At the law office his partner, Morris, sometimes found him staring into space or out the window. At one point Morris commented that Morrisey must be in love, and when he responded by blushing, Morris' suspicions were confirmed. When Morrisey related the office incident to Theresa, her multiple and diverse reaction epitomized how she liked and didn't like his attention, how she wanted his respect and concern for her as a person, but felt awkward, uncomfortable and could not enjoy or accept his compliments. Morrisey attempted to discover Theresa's own feeling, which forced her to admit that she was afraid of being loved. It was totally foreign to her. It made her vulnerable and she couldn't cope with the possibility of wanting someone to love her and then of losing that love.

Did James's love ultimately win out? Was the power of his love able to transform Theresa, to change her low self-image into an acceptance of her own value? Were they, at the novel's conclusion, married and living happily ever after?

Unfortunately, the answer to all these questions is "no."

On one particularly painful occasion Theresa hurt James deeply by a remark in which she made herself out to be worse than she was and intentionally unfaithful to him. The lawyer, deeply troubled, left her and avoided seeing or calling her for a time. But when he next telephoned he asked her to marry him. Theresa simply couldn't handle that. The absence of sexual attraction for him combined with her own confused inner feelings and self-hatred left the woman torn by his request and indecisive in responding.

In the midst of that uncertainty, she returned to her old hangout, the local tavern called Mr. Goodbar, picked up a stranger and, after an evening's sexual episode, was brutally murdered.

Despite the tragic ending, James Morrisey, in many ways, did at least partially succeed. His love was able to move Theresa, but her inability to accept love kept her from becoming a whole, integrated, happy person.

Don Quixote's deep and worshiping love for the prostitute Aldonza was more successful. He gave her a new name and his love transformed the woman's own self-image. Music from that production speaks of dreaming the impossible dream and describes the harlot's transformation.

The playing of Dulcinea was another of those powerful moments on my weekend. Familiar with that melody, I nevertheless found its meaning in this context seemed so much richer. A single concept kept reverberating throughout my being: the transforming power of love; the ability of one person's love, like that of Don Quixote, to change, lift up, transform another individual.

This idea, I suppose, has always been the font of inspiration behind my generous deeds and ultimately, no doubt, the reason for selecting priesthood with its companion, celibacy.

Honest friends, too, the kind who tell the truth and not simply flatter, also have indicated I have been a giving person in life, perhaps more generous than some. But those same individuals would observe that I find it difficult to accept love, that I hold myself aloof, and maintain a certain protective wall which keeps people at a distance.

Why? Is it a deep down poor self-image? A naturally reserved temperament? An effort to conform to some role of the priest which says he must hold back and always be under control? My seminary training? The modern male mystique with the tough inner guy à la John Wayne as its model? A fear of being vulnerable or dependent?

The reasons are neither clear nor important. However, for me the inspiration from Dulcinea was to give more of that love; it didn't speak to me about my own inability and need to accept love. That didn't surface strongly on my original Marriage Encounter. But it came during the days, even hours, which followed and greatly clarified at the team-training experience.

On the first weekend, my major concern was how to cope with those 50 encountered couples waiting for me at the potluck, welcome home supper. Throughout the 44 hours I thought and verbalized: Will I cry? Must I fake feelings of enthusiasm with them? How about the hugging and kissing? What will my reactions be?

The return home and that celebration in the church hall made it clear I was being moved and taught more profoundly on the weekend than I realized. There were tears, unashamed ones; there was genuine, not artificial enthusiasm; there were embraces, but these came out of an intensity of inner feeling which could express itself only in nonverbals; there was an enormous spirit of joy among all those present. When I stood to give a little speech of appreciation for their prayers and sacrifices, the words stuck in my throat and I had to stop with my impromptu talk unfinished.

That moment of frustration seemed to bring the entire process together. For the first time these loving parishioners were seeing the real me. The barriers dropped; the shell opened up; the heart was exposed; the tight grip let go. As one person commented: "You have always loved us, but we could never love you back. You never let us love you. Now we know you understand our love for you and that makes us very happy."

This is a marvelously intricate and mysterious process—the mutual interplay of loving persons. In a way, these statements sound terribly naive and excessively simple, maybe to some, corny. But the happiness jointly experienced and its continuation under a variety of situations over many months is certainly real.

This joy contrasts with some of the hidden, painful, unexpressed aloneness or loneliness I felt before Marriage Encounter.

On one occasion I had been visiting a dying non-Catholic whose family were parishioners. The response on this man's part was positive, but there were no indications of his desire to embrace the Church. He did, however, a few days later so respond to the efforts of another priest.

Afterwards, one of the relatives mentioned that the man held me in such high regard, a sort of awe, that he was afraid to approach me and preferred to turn to another priest for his conversion. I felt no deep jealousy here and truly rejoiced over the good done. Twenty years in the priesthood has taught me how infinitely unique are the ways God works through different priests. But I experienced a sadness: what is this distance, aloofness which causes some people to stay away or fear to reach out and ask my help?

Another example. After a lecture in another city, I was invited to the home of some personal acquaintances. After being the performer for three hours, I really wanted to unwind and share some of my personal self with this couple. Having followed the purely functionary model for eight busy years of speaking, working, lecturing, I had allowed almost no time for this kind of relationship and was evidently starved for it.

Upon arriving at the house, I found my well-intentioned friends had asked two other couples, who were strangers, to come and meet "the famous lecturer." I felt immediately drained and frustrated. This was more of the same—performing my function, keeping up appearances. After a brief half hour, I excused myself on the grounds of fatigue and drove home. I remember well the pain of that night's journey: wanting some closeness or intimacy, but finding the door closed; judging with a certain sad resignation that this must be the cost of being busy and well known. I prayed with a pained confusion, "Lord, I guess you just don't want this sort of support and close relationships for me."

A final illustration. The farewell party for a person I had worked with brought some feelings (and subtle remarks) of envy on my part. I judged he had not worked as hard or probably as effectively as I had with these same people. Yet they were giving him such a warm send-off.

The jealous feelings confused and troubled me, even caused a bit of guilt. Later, after Marriage Encounter, I realized the source of my difficulty.

I had perhaps loved more than he. But he allowed these people to love him. Since at that point my circle of protection was still impregnable, I felt again the sense of isolation and aloneness. I really wanted people to love and be close to me, but simply did not understand what the price tag was for that.

Marriage Encounter taught me that the premium was not necessarily more giving love, but an openness which would allow others to love me.

All this may sound as if I have been deprived of love in my life and understand little of God or other people's love for me. That is not the case. My family has always been loving and supportive. In addition, parishioners in every assignment have displayed their care frequently and in many different ways.

Moreover, I have reflected frequently in prayer on such phrases as this key one from St. John's Gospel: "As the Father has loved me, so I have loved you. Live on in my love" (Jn 15:9).

The late and saintly Benedictine Dom Damasus Winzen, founder and prior of Mount Savior Monastery near Elmira, New York, at two crucial periods of my ministry simply repeated to me his favorite remark: "The love of God for us is constant. Only we can keep it from reaching our hearts."

But to a certain extent that understanding of being loved by God and others seemed to remain in my head and not reach my heart. I knew this, but the realization had somehow not penetrated my total being.

Marriage Encounter and its aftermath seemed to achieve that. At least these couples gave me a greater awareness of what it means to be loved; they brought much happiness into my own heart and, apparently, if I can believe their testimony, caused me to drop that protective, isolating circle which had surrounded me.

The encountered couples with their eager readiness to express those feelings and articulate the truths behind them were, in a sense, the James Morrisey and Don Quixote of my life. Their love achieved a beginning transformation in me. But this did not stop with and remain an exclusive Marriage Encounter experience. It simultaneously leapt over into my relationships with all other parishioners.

These are admittedly intangible elements difficult to measure or assess. In the final analysis only the parishioners can give that evaluation. But I sense a greater joy and excitement in our parish now; I feel closer to my people; I believe they, too, are more comfortable and open, thus much happier with me as well.

7

Signs of Love

The *Ms.* magazine writers and readers are not particularly fond of St. Paul. Neither does the National Organization of Women (NOW) usually introduce their sessions with a quote from one of his epistles. Certainly, modern advocates of women's liberation would not cite the following excerpt from his letter to the Ephesians as their favorite biblical text.

> Defer to one another out of reverence for Christ. Wives should be submissive to their husbands as if to the Lord because the husband is head of his wife just as Christ is head of his body the church, as well as its savior. As the church submits to Christ, so wives should submit to their husbands in everything.
>
> Husbands, love your wives, as Christ loved the church. He gave himself up for her to make her holy, purifying her in the bath of water by the power of the word, to present himself a glorious church, holy and immaculate, without stain or wrinkle or anything of that sort. Husbands should love their wives as they do their own bodies. He who loves his wife loves himself. Observe that no one ever hates his own flesh; no, he nourishes it and takes care of it as Christ cares for the church—for we are members of his body.

> "For this reason a man shall leave his father
> and mother,
> and shall cling to his wife,
> and the two shall be made into one."

This is a great foreshadowing; I mean that it refers to Christ and the church. In any case, each one should love his wife as he loves himself, the wife for her part showing respect for her husband (Eph 5:21-33).

This same passage, however, serves as a pivotal, fundamental basis for the theology and practice of Marriage Encounter.

In a way, the two movements, Marriage Encounter and Women's Liberation, are strange bedfellows.

For example, most NOW personnel find this teaching from Ephesians abhorrent, contrary to their goals and demeaning to women. Some of the most bitter critics of my writings have directed their hostility toward the inclusion of that text in the Marriage preparation booklet, *Together for Life.*

On the other hand, Marriage Encounter finds no problem with the passage properly understood and sees in it a rich teaching on the true relationship between husband and wife.

Opposed as the movements are in this regard, they at least on the surface seem to unite in a concerted effort to discourage false stereotype roles for the man and woman in marriage. Women's Liberation, for example, insists the wife need not feel she is only a housekeeper and home-builder. It would recommend a career for her, greater independence and a marriage contract to divide domestic duties.

Marriage Encounter similarly urges a greater sharing of responsibilities, believes the husband should communicate his office problems with the wife, and urges a mother to share the family tasks with her spouse.

I would be cautious, nevertheless, in pursuing a deeper parallel between the two movements.

Marriage Encounter sets as its primary objective the unity and closeness of a married couple. God's plan, it maintains, is this: "A man . . . shall cling to his wife, and the two shall be made into one" (Eph 5:31). To promote that oneness and facilitate growth of such a closeness through the technique called dialogue is the essence of the encounter movement.

The world's plan for couples, on the contrary, as we have seen, is for them to live, practically speaking, as "married singles," each one in so many ways going a separate path.

To aid in achieving God's plan for marriage, the close union of spouses, Marriage Encounter seeks to foster a sensitive sharing of feelings between husband and wife with dialogue the pragmatic tool to accomplish that exchange.

Despite the two-in-one-flesh physical unity of man and woman, they remain distinct and unique individuals. Every one of us is a singular person, separate and apart from others. Moreover, each human being exists as a special creation of God.

That specialness manifests itself in a variety of ways: no two physical bodies are exactly alike; the thoughts I possess and the judgments or decisions I make in daily life likewise reflect my individuality; but my feelings, according to the Marriage Encounter view, especially express that uniqueness. They tell who I truly am; they reach to the core of my entire being.

When couples (or a priest and his people) are able mutually to share feelings, an enormous sense of oneness, of closeness, develops and with that a corresponding joy and satisfaction.

Particularly marvelous and mysterious in such an

interchange is the fact that I do not lose my own identity in the process. Marriage Encounter principles maintain I am not less myself because I have shared how I feel. Nor is there any lessening of that feeling I have just given to the other nor any diminution of my own feeling through the taking on of another's.

In the couple's dialogue, a partner does not give in or give up to the other, but simply gives. Each spouse shares and seeks to understand.

We experience the same phenomenon in love (dialogue on feelings is actually but a form of love and should be done lovingly). A popular motto rather accurately states that love is not love until you give it away. My love is not decreased in the least by sharing it with another. The opposite holds true; it increases through the giving. Joys are doubled and burdens halved by sharing, the saying goes.

Couples fresh from a weekend and enthusiastic about this new awareness of God's plan for their special oneness sometimes slip into an exaggerated approach. "From now on we will do everything together!" That idealistic pair have lost sight, temporarily at least, of their individual uniqueness and their singular specialness before God.

After a talk I presented on the sacrament of Penance in Houston, a young married and just-encountered couple came to me with this question: "Father, what do you think about a couple confessing together?"

I hesitated to dampen the eagerness of this hand-holding pair before me, but honesty required me to say: "I don't think it is a very wise practice."

Both their heads dropped with disappointment.

I went on to explain that this procedure ignored the mysterious uniqueness of each person, falsely presumed that the oneness or closeness of marriage meant surrendering individual identities, and could eventually lead to disastrous consequences.

"Right now, after Marriage Encounter, you have no difficulty with a joint confession. But later, for any number of reasons, one of you may not wish to receive the sacrament. The other could then become suspicious or mistrusting."

The youthful husband agreed. "Honey, Father's right. The other day you wanted to go, but I didn't and it had nothing to do with you or our relationship."

A veteran encountered wife supplied me with another illustration of this false tendency to overemphasize in daily living a couple's togetherness.

Two visitors, both strong supporters of Marriage Encounter, commented to her on how, following their weekends, they had ceased to fulfill several functions in the parish because they could not perform them as a couple.

The hostess disagreed.

"My husband and I have not lost our special gifts from God because of our newfound togetherness in Marriage Encounter. We are able to do some things as a couple—lector on Sundays at Mass, for example. But I cannot serve at this time as a minister of Communion; he can. My husband is not gifted with an ability to teach religion to third-graders; I think I am. We are both using our own personal and unique talents for building up the Church."

Marriage Encounter sees in that closeness and the total giving of a couple a reflection of the love, unity and total giving of the Holy Trinity and of Jesus' love for the Church.

St. Paul's words to the Ephesians are pertinent here:

"This is a great foreshadowing; I mean that it refers to Christ and the Church" (5:32).

"Husbands, love your wives, as Christ loved the Church" (5:25).

"As the Church submits to Christ, so wives should submit to their husbands in everything" (5:24).

The original weekend presents to couples this statement for their reflection: "Three and two are one." It means: "Three persons are one God, one love relationship, and two persons are one couple, one love relationship." The similarity rests in the oneness of the love relationship which exists both in the Trinity and between a couple.

It has been very customary for priests to use an analogous equation for the sacrament of Matrimony and to view the wedding ceremony as a triangle. Three are involved, according to this approach, in the celebration: God, the bride and the groom. The priest simply stands as a witness. The couple actually administer the sacrament to each other and the Lord cements their union.

Marriage Encounter deeply impresses upon couples the sacramental or sign value of their relationship. Thus, it should mirror the closeness and love of the Trinity and of Jesus' love for the Church; but it also can lead others to a better awareness of the Father, Son and Holy Spirit and the love present within the Godhead.

In my ministry I have seen this often verified with engaged couples. A nonpracticing Catholic or half-believing partner, for example, will, through the love experience with a future spouse, somehow rediscover the existence of God and the importance of the Lord in his or her life.

Similarly today, couples on a Marriage Encounter weekend frequently through a renewal of their nuptial closeness find themselves drawing nearer to God. In fact, they later discover an intimate connection between these two facets of their lives. What builds up their relationship with the Father, strengthens their marital bond;

what deepens their marriage closeness, enhances their oneness with our Lord.

In that context, St. Paul's words to the Ephesians appear to offer no obstacle for the contemporary Marriage Encounter couple. The relationships sketched there are not seen as demeaning. Instead, the emphasis stressed is that of serving each other, giving, respecting, reaching out, being close. Liberation critics seem to concentrate on the submissive note and fail to catch the richer dimension of that passage.

On my deeper weekend I heard eloquent testimonies on the mutual impact of a couple's relationship with God and with each other.

One wife said to her husband: "Before Marriage Encounter, I believed in God, but called on him only in emergencies. It was the same with you. I was close to you, but only called on you when I needed you. Marriage Encounter changed that."

A husband observed: "We were both products of Catholic schools, always went to church and prayed. But God was separate to each one of us. We never prayed together. Even after Vatican II we kept up to date on the Church. Following Marriage Encounter we discovered a new relationship. We now pray out loud together. Marriage Encounter brought the two of us and God together."

These are the real-life illustrations of a theoretical point made on my original weekend. "As a couple you are a sacrament: a sign and symbol of God's presence in the world, of his love for us. Your love for one another is a sign and symbol of this."

8

Talking with Our Father

An urban Catholic couple in their 20's began to slip after the wedding into an unfortunately typical, modern American religious stance. Baptized and raised as members of the Church, they still believed, but had ceased participating in Sunday Mass.

When their first baby arrived, they called at the rectory to arrange for this infant's Baptism. The priest, when informed they hadn't been at Sunday liturgies, asked: "Are you Catholics?" The husband and wife replied, "Why, yes. We were raised Catholics and believe in the Church or we wouldn't be here. We just don't go to Mass." The priest countered with, "Well, then, you aren't really Catholics." A long and heated discussion ensued, with the priest finally and somewhat reluctantly agreeing to baptize the child.

Later this couple made a Marriage Encounter, and, in their own words, "found God and the Church."

Monday morning following their weekend, the husband's first stop out of the house was at the rectory. He inquired for the priest, apologized to him, and mentioned that he now understood what the man was attempting to communicate in their earlier animated and somewhat unpleasant argument. The husband and wife have not missed a Sunday Mass since their encounter.

Within a few months they invited that priest to their house for dinner. As all sat down at the table, the guest immediately took up knife and fork and began to eat. The husband then suggested:

"Father, would you mind if we pray first?"

He smiled sheepishly, felt foolish as everyone does in such a situation, put down his silverware, prayed with them, and stayed until 1:00 a.m.

Most couples do not arrive at a Marriage Encounter hoping or expecting to find God and the Church. Nor is that the main thrust of the presentations nor even the direct object of the weekend. But as we mentioned in the last chapter, a connection does exist between the couple's relationship with each other and their relationship with God. Moreover, countless testimonies like that of this young urban husband and wife speak of the positive religious impact Marriage Encounter has actually exercised on couples.

Encountered and dialoguing couples seem to develop a much more personal approach to God and prayer; in particular, they become more aware of the Lord as a warm and loving Father.

The presenting husband on my original weekend spoke about a change in his attitude toward God after their weekend. He found the Lord not so impersonal but part of his daily life—a loving Father involved in the relationships he has with his wife and others.

The wife commented in a similar vein. She now feels surer of her faith, closer to God, secure in her relationship with the Lord and able to converse much more informally with the Father in heaven.

On my team-training session, a husband remarked:

Prior to Marriage Encounter, the only time I said "God" was before "damn it." Then we were called to be a team couple. I thought to myself, "This has to be a mistake!" Through many years of Catholic education God always meant sad, not happy things to me. After the weekend, God was like an old friend you hadn't seen for years and years. I now go to church, the children's Mass, and like it. I feel like saying, "Hi, God!" God has become a friend and I talk to him all day long.

This sudden ability or confidence to talk with God all day long and to pray publicly, spontaneously, vocally to the Father with others is one of the more remarkable transformations I have observed in myself and among our encountered parishioners.

Prior to my own Marriage Encounter, I joined six or seven encountered spouses for a Sunday night dinner, welcoming home one of our team couples who had just given their initial weekend. As we sat down for dinner, all joined hands and our host asked the team husband to say grace.

It was not the usual, "Bless us, O Lord. . ." Instead he prayed out loud in thanksgiving for the weekend, for these supportive couples and for the food. A few others added petitions to the Father or words of gratitude. Then a joint "Amen" from all.

Several points struck me. First, no one automatically requested "Father" to give the blessing. This was no put-down of myself, but simply a recognition of their own dignity, competence and right as baptized Christians to lead people on occasion in prayer. Secondly, these couples were not awkward or self-conscious joining hands. Thirdly, they had so grown in an awareness of their relationship to the Father that these words flowed naturally and genuinely from both hearts and lips.

I have known each of these couples for over five years. They all were and are extremely active in the parish, generous with their time, and weekly, even daily communicants. But Marriage Encounter and a few short months of dialoguing brought about this richer dimension to their religious lives.

These people are now so comfortable with themselves and with the Father that they likewise do not hesitate to pray in a public setting. In this regard their simplicity and softly apostolic approach could shame some of us who, as sophisticated priests or religious, may skip grace in an elegant restaurant or mumble private prayers on planes lest those around us notice.

Several encountered couples took me to the airport as I left for the team-training weekend. When departure time arrived, one husband suggested we form a "prayer circle" and ask the Father's help. Despite the crowded lobby, no one of the group seemed to mind. We spoke briefly and directly, but openly to God about my approaching trip and session.

After the plane took off, the couples went to the airport restaurant for dinner. They ordered drinks and, a few moments later, decided to offer grace. Once again, hands were joined and soft, heartfelt words rose to the Father. The waitress, meanwhile, had returned, stopped and was quite stunned by this apparently normal, but unusually joyous group praying in that public spot.

True conversation with another is a two-way experience, a dialogue, not a monologue. Talking with our Father thus also involves listening as well as speaking.

We believe as Catholics, of course, that God's words for us are found in the Church's living tradition and the written texts of the bible. Marriage Encounter makes much of both and considers scripture as a love letter from the Lord and from those faithful Christians who have lived since the days of Jesus.

On the side of our seminary building here at the North American College in Rome are carved, in Latin, words from the breviary, the Church's official prayer book.

Roughly translated they say: "O happy Rome, you have been made holy by the glorious blood of your two leaders." That reference is to St. Peter and St. Paul whose martyred blood has watered the soil of this city.

Through the centuries many have followed the path of those two men and by their lives handed down to us the Christian heritage. Similarly, the written word of God in scripture is actually a living document, the product of countless persons who have transmitted these inspired texts to us. Some died for its truths; others taught the message; additional ones copied the manuscripts or printed the books; still others interpreted those biblical words and, today, a vast army of preachers and teachers proclaims its good news.

On my original weekend I was impressed to hear the team husband speak with enthusiasm and awe of the bible as a love letter from the Father. Before Marriage Encounter he admitted skipping Mass now and then. Today he carefully listens to the readings during the liturgy and usually discovers something which applies to his life. Moreover, when he reads on his own, this husband finds the words now almost leap out at him from the page.

In their personal dialogues, couples frequently will read a passage of scripture beforehand or actively write on the feelings which arise from a particular excerpt.

This latter procedure can be especially helpful for priests and religious during what is termed a scripture dialogue. According to that practice, an individual selects the night before a passage in which the Lord or his message stands out with some clarify and force. The next day, this person prepares for the dialogue by holding the scriptures in his or her hand and seeking to become present to all the people of that book.

After a prayer to our Father for an awareness of what is involved here (my sinfulness, God's love for me, the experience of the Church), the individual opens up the bible to the passage previously selected.

Having made the scene clearly and vividly present, the person then writes a love letter to the Father in response to the question: "How are you, Jesus, making me feel in speaking this way to me now?"

What normally follows is a series of intervals alternating between writing and reflecting, with the essential purpose not to put myself down on paper, but to experience my relationship with the Father and his Son, Jesus.

I have found the theologians preparing for priesthood in this seminary quite comfortable with that notion of talking to the Father. Very biblically oriented people, they pray spontaneously with skill and sincerity.

The last characteristic is, naturally, the key quality. One sometimes senses that an open prayer has become a speech or is a conversation with others present, not a word spoken directly to the Father. To achieve this genuineness requires, in my experience, great concentration and an alert awareness of what is being done at that moment.

Our American Bishops have encouraged seminarians, as part of their preparation for the ecumenical dimension of the ministry, "to develop the habit of spontaneous vocal prayer, a type of prayer that is familiar to Protestants."[1]

That training and ultimate skill will, in addition, help them relate more successfully to the Marriage Encounter couples who both speak with and listen to our Father in heaven.

---

[1] National Conference of Catholic Bishops. *The Program of Priestly Formation.* Washington: Publications Office, 1976. p. 72.

9
Sex and Death

Roman Catholics whose marriages have ended up in divorce courts or who fall in love with individuals married previously have more hope today.

Up to a decade ago, Church annulments of most marriages were rarely granted; they demanded enormously complicated testimonies and required years for completion. Thanks to simplified, but still thorough procedures in many dioceses of the United States, persons with broken marital bonds have the possibility of obtaining a decree of nullity usually within 12 months.

These annulments are not automatic, nor do they only superficially examine the case under question. The procedures vary from place to place, but ordinarily this process entails a lengthy written questionnaire from one partner, several supportive witnesses and a formal hearing before Church matrimonial specialists as well as a psychologist.

One unmarried Catholic woman soon will be able to wed her non-Catholic fiance in a Church ceremony because his previous nuptial bond has been annulled through one of these procedures. In writing about the experience, she offers an interesting comment on at least the surface attitude toward sex of the matrimonial court personnel:

> We had the hearing with the marriage tribunal and John was granted his annulment. He was a nervous wreck the day of the hearing. His jokes about an impending interrogation complete with electric chair, tape recorder, torture, etc., seemed to help him, but not me. I'm glad there was one non-clerical member on the court. The psychologist wasn't a priest, so John found someone to identify with. It definitely helped when they questioned him about his past sexual life in marriage. He was reassured that the psychologist sympathized with him. . . I wish priests and sisters were better trained to handle the reality that sex is part of life.

The originators of Marriage Encounter theorized and the experiences of those many weekends since its inception have confirmed that married couples are often equally uncomfortable with their sexuality. Not just priests and sisters get red-faced or look at the floor.

One wife on a weekend observed to her husband: "I am not very happy with my own body. If you touch me in a place I am not proud of, I tend to say this doesn't please me."

Another commented to her spouse:

> I was brought up a good Catholic girl who was never to wear patent leather shoes, knew nothing about sex and didn't talk about it. You made me the lover, the sexual partner I am. I now have no inhibitions, no bad feelings about sex.

The biblical teaching, "God looked at everything he had made, and he found it very good" (Gn 1:31), seems to have been forgotten by many or certainly not applied by them to the area of sex.

The weekend does not give a lengthy presentation

on the what, why and how of sex in marriage. It offers no earthy description of infallible techniques. These are readily available, although questionably helpful, at newsstands and bookstores.

But Marriage Encounter does facilitate communication between spouses on this, probably the most difficult area of their relationship to discuss. Simply coming to grips with each other's feelings about sex seems to eliminate negative attitudes, to make clear the scriptural text quoted above and to promote a joyfulness in sexual relationships not previously present.

> I was taught sex is dirty, bad, a wife's duty. Nice girls don't enjoy it. I wouldn't have sex during the daytime because I was ashamed to have you see me. But after Marriage Encounter I was no longer afraid. One of our greatest experiences was an afternoon of joy I am now carrying with me.

If you were asked what are the two most problematic topics for a married couple to discuss, I am sure the first answer would be "sex." That answer is correct. But the other?

Few persons ever mention the subject "death" in response to such an inquiry. However, this appears to be for the vast majority of couples (and single individuals as well) the second most painful, uncomfortable, difficult, never-to-be-mentioned or talked about issue.

"The possibility of life without you frightens me beyond description."

"I can't think of life here without each other, even though I know we will have life forever in heaven."

Those two testimonies speak both of the deep marital love present and an almost correspondingly anxious fear of death.

It should be no surprise that death and dying are taboo topics for couples. Most people avoid mention of the word and certainly discussion of the subject.

In a book often quoted today, *On Death and Dying,* Dr. Elizabeth Kubler-Ross outlined five stages of reaction usually experienced by a terminally ill patient and his or her family.

The first stage she terms denial and isolation. When we drive by a serious accident, the unconscious reaction generally runs like this: "Too bad. What a pity. But that never would happen to *me*."

Five years ago I was circling over the North Philadelphia airport in a commuter airplane with two pilots and a dozen other passengers. The wheels were locked up inside the fuselage and we flew around and around for one hour in preparation for an emergency landing.

In the beginning, one automatically believes the plane will get down (it will, but not necessarily the way you want). Only as time passes does the realization sink in that possibly you will crash, you will die, this is the end. There was a crash but, fortunately for us, no one died or was injured, and it wasn't the end.

Dr. Kubler-Ross maintains every terminally infirm patient experiences this denial stage. In her mind, it helps the sick person initially to face a fatal, desperate and uncontrollable situation. We can't change that destiny, so we pretend it doesn't exist or tell ourselves the problem will go away. We also look to others for confirmation of our denial.

"I am feeling better today, Father. Expect to be home and at Mass within a week or two." You know he will be in church soon, but probably for his funeral.

"Nurse, don't you think I look improved this morning?"

"Doctor, I see they have a new drug for this disease. . . ."

That denial often leads to or is accompanied by a stage of isolation. The patient withdraws, becomes silent, loses interest or wants no visitors, prefers to think alone.

Immediately after my mother's funeral, I wasn't up to visiting with all the relatives for a brief period of time. I went upstairs and needed to be alone with my grief.

That very isolation, however, can produce a further, deeper loneliness. We can contribute to this by avoiding the dying person because of our own anxiety or inadequacy in the face of death.

Not only human nature as it tries to cope with death, but modern culture and society contribute to this denial of one's demise. From artificial grass covering the mound of loose earth beside a grave to euphemistic words such as "he left us," "she passed on," the world seeks to ease the pain or hide the reality of our eventual end.

Once again, the Marriage Encounter weekend does not treat death directly by a lengthy presentation on the subject. But it does raise the topic and lead couples into an important communication on this most thorny area. They are thus asked to share with each other awkward, previously hidden feelings. That takes confidence, a loving trust in the other, which we will now discuss.

10

Confidence: Key to Sharing, Caring and Confronting

When seventh-grader Tom came home one evening, his parents suspected that something was troubling the boy. He walked around distracted with that half-interested, half-bored kind of attitude. They suspected that the boy wanted to share an experience or concern with them, but couldn't quite get it out.

They were right. Tom did have something to share.

The love bug had bitten him. At least he felt for the first time in that young life some very warm, but unusual feelings for a girl his age. He wished to talk over with dad and mom these strange emotions swirling inside him, but a certain fear held him back.

Would his parents scold him? Make fun of him? Put him down?

Those were confused, inarticulated anxieties. But they kept him silent and at a distance.

At the same moment, however, another force, equally inarticulated and uncertain, urged him to get the matter out into the open. Share this with your parents, it suggested. Trust them. Have confidence in their love for you. Remember how in earlier times they have accepted you, your feelings, your thoughts, your actions. They will do so again.

The second voice gradually won out. Recollection of past loving acceptances gave him courage.

At first, he indirectly hinted at what was on his mind. When the parents did not puncture that trial balloon, but held it gently in their hands, Tom felt an infusion of trust and confidence. More came out. Then more and more and more.

This revelation of a difficult inner feeling resulted not so much from Tom's personal courage as from the trust and confidence he placed in his parents. He made a decision to believe in their goodness and love. The boy judged their concern for him would lead mom and dad to accept his feelings and not ridicule them.

Young Tom felt good and close to his parents afterwards. He had allowed them to love him. Similarly, the son's trust and confidence in their goodness and love warmed the father and the mother's hearts.

Marriage Encounter calls this confidence the key to dialogue. It views trust or confidence as a decision (not a feeling) to believe my partner is lovable enough, full of sufficient goodness to accept me as I am. Because of the good qualities I see and have experienced in you, I decide to entrust you with a particularly difficult feeling I am afraid or embarrassed to share.

After Marriage Encounter, I personally revealed those awkward ambitious feelings mentioned earlier with a team couple I trusted or in whom I had that confidence. Soon afterwards, however, it was also possible for me to exchange these, from a different angle, with perhaps my closest priest friend.

Why was I now able to do so? Probably for a variety of reasons: less concern about upholding my previous image of the perfect priest; an awareness of the confidence-trust decision involved in communication; a deeper appreciation of his goodness; a willingness to let him love and accept me for what I am.

This type of confidence and the sharing which it makes possible is not the same as confession. In my years as a priest I have frequently visited with a guilty present or future married partner who felt compelled to reveal all to the other.

That may seem honest and open, but Marriage Encounter questions its wisdom. This merely transfers a burden which only God can lift from one person's shoulder to the other. As a team priest mentioned: if the wronged spouse becomes angry and unforgiving, the guilty partner then can feel the deed was justified from the beginning; if the offended partner, on the other hand, is very accepting and understanding, the culpable spouse may believe it was not such a bad action after all.

At the first information night I attended, a husband remarked that on his weekend he went to confession for the first time in eight years. When this penitent partner approached a priest for the sacrament, he said, "Do you want your wife to come along?"

I was puzzled by that suggestion and, as I remarked before, inwardly not much in agreement with the practice. Apparently that event must have been either in the initial Marriage Encounter days or the result of misguided enthusiasm on the part of an inexperienced team priest. Present guidelines and current leaders rather clearly indicate such a procedure should not be encouraged.

This type of couple confession not only fails to recognize the uniqueness of an individual person, it also obscures what Marriage Encounter means by the confidence required in dialogue. The weekend stresses that this is not garbage dumping, nor the revelation of some action or event (that would be confession), but the decision to be more honest and open with my beloved.

The wife described at the conclusion of Chapter three who, on a Sunday morning of her weekend, made a confidence decision to express feelings never before discussed with her husband, experienced a joyful surprise. Because of his goodness, she trustingly shared difficult inner sentiments with him. However, before he had a chance for response to her note, she was reading his love letter with its enormous outpouring of love for this woman. He, in turn, had recognized such immense goodness within his wife that it encouraged him to make a confidence decision of his own. The detailed and explicit expression of his deep love for her certainly at that point must have been a difficult sharing for him.

That woman's task now is to believe in the good image he possesses of her and not to dwell or accept the poor self-image she has struggled with for so long.

The students at the North American College have a marvelous tradition of welcoming guests for the noon main meal with a standing enthusiastic ovation.

I have watched the joy and tears it can bring to the recipient's heart and eyes. One couple celebrating their 15th wedding anniversary simply sat during the applause with bowed heads and blushing faces. An older woman, the mother of a faculty member, reached for a handkerchief to stem the stream flowing down her cheeks. A popular seminarian just returned from the United States and the burial of his father, stood awkwardly, but with a smile of happiness and content, grateful to be so warmly accepted back into the family.

Nearly every day we likewise sing birthday congratulations to the celebrating individual. That person's reaction will speak a bit about his own ability to accept compliments and possibly even reveal a portion of his comfortable or uncomfortable, high or low self-image.

When one venerable and beloved scholar arrived at the seminary for a temporary stay of some months, he was impressed and enthused by the thunderous reception accorded him. On the next day, however, a similar, although probably lesser ovation was extended to that meal's visitors. The older scholar's previous joy immediately soured, he made a few grumbling remarks and would never join in the applause during his ensuing weeks at the seminary.

His colleagues and the students deeply loved this man and thus with great, gentle kindness still laughingly describe the irked professor's sudden disenchantment. It was clearly a failing on his part—he had slipped into the trap of comparing, of matching his accolade with another's. In that process a person always loses. Instead of viewing the other's gift or goodness as something beautiful in itself and from God, I see that trait in competition with my own talents and thus judge it a threat to or a diminishing of myself.

I found this an enormously positive effect of Marriage Encounter for me and for the others returning from weekends. We did not become instant saints, naturally, but there seemed a greater readiness to praise others, a better ability or willingness to recognize goodness in my neighbor, a deeper reluctance to speak uncharitably or to mention negative points about some person.

During my many priest retreats, I often made resolutions to act in this fashion, only to return home and discover my life pattern remained the same. This was not the case after Marriage Encounter. After a retreat I *knew* that I *should* be more kind and less negative, more praising and less jealous, but a strong part of me didn't want to respond in this fashion. Following my weekend, I felt, on the contrary, an uncanny inner attitude which made me *want* to see goodness in others and *want* to avoid the least bit of conversation which dwelt on a neighbor's fault.

In time some of that interior feeling diminished, but even now, a year later, I am more keenly aware of the situation. When I catch myself slipping back into one of those comparing, self-centered, negative moods, it appears easier to snap out of them by concentrating on the goodness I see in the other.

That approach also helps us to be more comfortable with persons whose backgrounds and life-styles vary greatly from our own. Here in this enormously international city, we run daily into people of various colors, individuals who speak and think and dress and act differently than we do.

There seems an innate tendency within us to judge, normally in an unconscious fashion, that those persons are inferior to us. For example, because she can't speak English, that woman is not as intelligent as I am (the fact is she speaks four languages and has a Ph.D.; I can't even speak Italian and have no degree). Or, because he has different ideas that man is not as orthodox or informed as I am (the fact is he has a much better background in today's theology than I do).

When we grow more confident in and comfortable with ourselves, then these threatened, superior, comparing attitudes begin to decrease. We see ourselves as special and unique before God; we have our own gifts and goodness. Others are equally unique and special with their own goodness and gifts. We look for and rejoice in those gifts, giving praise to the Lord for his blessings on us and in those individuals.

St. Paul surely encourages that type of approach:

> Never let evil talk pass your lips; say only the good things men need to hear, things that will really help them. Do nothing to sadden the Holy Spirit with whom you were sealed against the day of redemption. Get rid of all bitterness, all passion and anger, harsh words, slander, and malice of every kind. In place of these be kind to one another, compassionate, and mutually forgiving, just as God has forgiven you in Christ (Eph 4:29-32).

Sometime after my weekend, I had a rather unpleasant confrontation with a priest colleague. We disagreed on a basic approach to some part of the ministry.

Prior to Marriage Encounter I tended to hold back such contrary opinions, retreat into a reserved, silent position which would conceal my own view and perhaps even give the other an impression I agreed, then later talk to a few friends about how I objected to this individual's statements.

I often would follow a similar pattern when hurt by what someone said or did. I never mentioned this to the offending person, yet normally discussed my pain later with several others.

This is hardly a courageous or ingenuous mode of behavior. However, it can be masked as the noble reactions of a quiet, reserved, sensitive, balanced, pleasant, agreeable, tolerant person.

My two weekends led me to believe the approach stemmed more from my poor self-image and the need consequently to have strong approval from others. With this strong urge to be popular, I thus hesitate to have someone disagree or be irked with me.

Marriage Encounter, in addition, appeared to deepen my awareness about the goodness of others and sharpen the desire to compliment or support my neighbor.

During this interchange with the priest, I objected to his approach (rather lovingly I believed), but pointed out several positive aspects of the work he had been doing. There were no bitter, hostile comments, just a forthright criticism of his methods in one area.

When we parted, his clammy handshake led me to judge that our exchange caused more pain and discomfort than I realized.

The next day our paths crossed and I remarked: "Sorry if our discussion yesterday caused you a lot of grief and anxiety."

He then called me aside and proceeded to vent his intense anger at what and how I had said the things I did. I kept calm (not the usual reaction in such an experience) but remained convinced of my opinion; I stood firm in opposition to his view, and, at the end, repeated my regret that our exchange had caused such pain.

"Pain, heck, I was really ticked off."

On my drive home I mulled the matter over and recognized how much Marriage Encounter had helped here.

First of all, I possessed now sufficient self-confidence to confront him. Secondly, the confrontation was carried on in a positive, loving way. Thirdly, I seemed much more sensitive to his pain. Fourthly, I was not so upset with his contrary view and consequent anger.

Normally, that final remark would have deeply troubled me and prompted several calls or visits looking for reassurance. I did not so react on this occasion. There was natural regret about the conflict and his displeasure. But inwardly I felt a conviction about the correctness of my stand and sensed a strength in being able to cope with the hostility expressed.

Unfortunately, I still do not always respond in such a manner. There remain some regressions to silence and cowardice, failures to confront, hesitations to object and tendencies to seek reassurance.

But these are less now than before. Moreover, the goal of loving confrontation based on confidence in myself, God and others stands before me. A daily dialogue with the Lord has helped keep that vision clearer in view and more operative in my life.

11

Who Is My Spouse?

Who is the priest's partner on a Marriage Encounter? Some attractive nun?

These half-joking, half-serious questions frequently arise in discussing a priest's relationship to the weekend. They were, also, personal anxieties within me prior to my original 44-hour experience.

I knew from earlier contact with veteran encountered personnel that there would be dialogues and love letters. But with whom? My closer priest friends were not interested or available for that weekend. Must it thus be with a strange priest? How would I react? Could I reveal my hidden self to a person I hardly knew?

The team priest on that Marriage Encounter was a young cleric of our diocese, but one I had not seen or talked to in many years. In fact, as Vocation Director I had interviewed him before his entrance into the seminary over a dozen years earlier.

When he remarked at the opening conference that the priest's spouse is the Church, the people of God, and I would be dialoging about my relationship with them, I felt like responding, "Sure. I know all that theology. But how and with whom?"

Perhaps I did know in my head this pre- and post-Vatican II theology about the nature of the Church as God's holy people, but I now begin to wonder if I really had grasped its significance in my heart. His reference to the Church as my spouse did not seem to register significantly at the start of the weekend nor even throughout the next two days.

However, as the months elapsed and especially during the team-training weekend, I came to a much more profound awareness of the implications behind having God's people as my spouse.

I described in an early section of this book the procedure by which priests are "coupled" for the deeper weekend so they do not prove a distraction for the married participants.

On the Sunday morning after breakfast, my partner left the dining hall a few minutes early and returned to our room for some personal business. As the rest of us rose from the tables, walked out of the cafeteria and headed up the hill for the dormitory, I commented to a young couple:

"Why don't you go on ahead together. Don't worry. I won't be lonely."

The wife turned, smiled and responded: "I know you won't, because you have a beautiful spouse!"

Her remark in that context seemed to piece together for me all those ideas about the priest, the people, the priesthood and the Church into a clear picture. Certainly that observation has remained fixed in my mind and I can recall it vividly here six months later.

Since my departure from the parish for Rome was then but a few weeks away, the comment took on special meaning for me.

Marriage Encounter has the power to heighten our own sensitivity toward feelings (my own and others) as well as to deepen a priest's relationships with parish-ioners. It thus made the pain of my leaving the people of Holy Family, even though for only 10 months, extremely acute and tearful. However, the wife's reminder shed a new light on the situation.

Reflection on this truth that the priesthood unites me to the universal Church, the entire Communion of Saints, the worldwide people of God, led me to grasp the practical ramifications of such a theology. It became evident that if I would but open myself in a loving way to the new persons soon to enter my life, the same type of joyful, close relationships surely must develop with them. The Lord's holy people live in Rome, Italy, as well as in Fulton, New York.

Three weeks after my arrival at the seminary in the Eternal City, I began to experience the validity of that approach and the apparent effect of Marriage Encounter on my inner life. I felt a tight bond already building up between myself and the students; in fact, I sensed that the farewell from them a few months later in June would involve the same pain I endured through the September severance from parishioners of Holy Family.

The young woman's clear vision of who my spouse is reflected her keen perception of that mystery which is the Church. Very evidently she and her husband had pondered in depth the passage of St. Paul to the Ephesians we cited above.

For the husband and wife to cling together, the two being made into one, "is a great foreshadowing; I mean that it refers to Christ and the Church" (Eph 5:31-32). This foreshadowing or mystery can be clarified when we "observe that no one ever hates his own flesh; no, he nourishes it and takes care of it as Christ cares for the church—for we are members of his body" (Eph 5:29).

Marriage Encounter translates those Pauline state-ments and the reference that "we are members of his body" into a simple, modern phrase: "We are the Church."

This declaration seems to open up new horizons for couples on a weekend. For the first time they appear to view the Church not as the Pope, the parish priest, the church building or the Catholic school, but as themselves. Their testimonies at the team-training session reflect that shift in understanding and attitude.

One husband observed: "Before Marriage Encounter I saw the Church as a physical structure. We went once a week with the kids, were seen by others and wasted an hour. I considered myself a Sunday Catholic, but it didn't mean much to me. After Marriage Encounter. . . I felt that by being one with other Catholics, I was one with God."

Another man commented: "The Church was a building. We were there, took the children, and received Communion. My wife taught CCD (religious instruction classes) and we thought we were good Catholics. How much our eyes have opened! Now we have such a yearning to be part of Sunday Mass. Before we found it difficult to sing; today we do so easily and loudly. I found it hard to pray and went to God only with a problem. Now I talk with the Lord every day on a regular basis. We now in prayer seek help for others and are less selfish. We include others in our needs and wants. We light a candle for them, think about them, pray for them."

Still a third spouse noted: "The Church was like a bible in every good Catholic home—there, but never opened up. Prior to Marriage Encounter the Church was there, but never really open to my life."

The acceptance of "We are the Church" has not, in my experience, led encountered persons to be anti-authoritarian, anticlerical, or antihierarchical. Their "we" includes priests, bishops and the Holy Father. But they do possess a new sense of their dignity and worth, of their essential importance to the Church.

All of this perfectly coincides with the teaching of the Fathers at the Second Vatican Council in their *Dogmatic Constitution on the Church,* article 11:

> Finally, in virtue of the sacrament of matrimony by which they signify and share (cf. Ephesians 5:32) the mystery of the unity and faithful love between Christ and the Church, Christian married couples help one another to attain holiness in their married life and in the rearing of their children. Hence by reason of their state in life and of their position they have their own gifts in the People of God (cf. 1 Corinthians 7:7). From the marriage of Christians there comes the family in which new citizens of human society are born and, by the grace of the Holy Spirit in baptism, those are made children of God so that the People of God may be perpetuated throughout the centuries. In what might be regarded as the domestic Church, the parents, by word and example, are the first heralds of the faith with regard to their children.[1]

To be a domestic Church, a miniature of the universal Church, a reflection of the mysterious link and love which exist between Christ and his Church—that is the vocation of a married couple and family.

They likewise serve as a sign and symbol for the sacrament of priesthood. Holy Orders has appointed me "to nourish the Church with the word and grace of God in the name of Christ."[2] As Christ loves the Church, his spouse, so must I love the Church, my spouse. But just as the love between husband and wife speaks of Christ's love for the Church, so their mutual bond tells me how much I should love them. And as the Church loves Christ, so couples ought to love me.

Marriage Encounter thus closely relates the two sacraments of Matrimony and priesthood or Holy Orders.

---

[1] *Vatican Council II,* general editor, Austin Flannery, O.P. Northport, New York: Costello Publishing Co., 1975, p. 362.
[2] *Ibid.*

Meditation upon Jesus' life in the Gospels can, of course, supply priests with inspiration and guidance for their ministry. The love of our Lord for his people leaps at us from every page. However, given the human, flesh-and-blood condition of this life, the here-and-now, specific, observable love of a couple for each other, of the couple for a priest and of the priest for his people sometimes may prove more supportive. I can see, hear, feel, taste, touch that human love. The divine love in biblical illustration and teachings is less tangible, sensible and therefore often harder to grasp.

Priests and married couples, in the Marriage Encounter view, consequently bear a responsibility to each other. They have a stake in each other's relationships. My love as a priest for you and others can help you grow as a couple. Your love for each other and for me helps me grow as a priest.

Prior to Marriage Encounter I never saw myself as a "clerical" priest. I loved, served and mixed with many, many fine people. They became part of my life, helped me in countless ways and dwell today in warm spots within my heart.

But deep down I think now there was a certain superiority feeling. I would visit their homes, yes, but always as one who is gracing the house with my presence; involve them in the parish, yes, but under my direction and control, however soft and subtle that might be; ask their advice, yes, but really reserve the final judgment to myself as one better equipped to make decisions.

The theology and practice of "We are the Church" have, I think, softened that attitude. Without in any way diminishing the priest's serious leadership responsibilities, this view of the Church does make him a bit more humble, more aware that he merely shares with others membership in the Lord's body. Moreover, the enormous growth I saw in the prayer life, charity, generosity and spiritual wisdom of these encountered couples—persons moving rapidly past and beyond me in many instances—led me to the realization of how much they and other lay persons have to teach me.

Relationships between the parish priest and his people are, of course, sometimes delicate and complex matters. We might even say that it is possible for the interchange to assume occasionally a certain toys and trophies aspect. Without any conscious malice or knowing manipulation, the priest may use married persons in a way as toys; they, on the other hand, may consider the priest as a kind of trophy.

The priest, for example, meets a pleasant couple or family, receives from them a warm reception, begins to visit their home and initiate a relationship. In time, the newness will wear off, their human side come forward and he may tire of that contact. Abandonment of them and a search elsewhere for another loving, supportive couple could be likened to a youngster who tires of one toy and places it back on the shelf, then takes up another for a period of time.

The couple or family, again in somewhat of a parallel, are proud to have the priest come to their home, offer their finest hospitality and afterwards share interesting aspects of the evening with friends or neighbors. In this context, the spouses, hardly aware of their motives or actions, may consider the priest a cherished trophy added to the family display case.

This is said not to discourage such priest-married persons contacts. It simply serves as a reminder of how all of us unconsciously can slip into the fault of manipulating others, of using people for our own needs and neglecting to love them purely as persons. When I have a stake in your life and you possess a similar investment in mine, we are called to an unselfish love of each other which rises above a toy or trophy approach.

At this point in my life I have found Marriage Encounter in general and dialogue with a couple in particular most helpful. A weekly experience of prayer, bible reading and dialogue with a mature husband and wife committed to the Church, wise in human relationships, involved with Marriage Encounter and dedicated to the Lord has been a source of great joy and, I believe, spiritual growth for me. We are aware, however, of the complications or misunderstandings which can arise through it for them, for me and for others.

12

Prayer and Fasting for Others

"Kevin, it's your time now!"

This was a mother's voice summoning home her sixth-grade son from a neighborhood pickup baseball game. The interchange which followed between Kevin and his companions, however, took a quite different turn from the usual, "Ah gee, do I have to? Well, see you later, guys." Instead it went something like this:

"Guys, I gotta go."
"Where you going?"
"I gotta do something."
"What d'ya gotta do?"
"I've gotta do something for church."
"For church!"
"I've gotta do something for Father Champlin."
"Oh." (A half-understanding, yet still-puzzled response.)
"I've gotta pray."

While rather self-conscious about the matter in the presence of his peers, Kevin still left the game, ran to his house, picked up the family bible and then read for five or 10 minutes.

This young man was fulfilling his part of a family prayer compact. During both my initial and team-training weekends, two Marriage Encounter families in the parish combined efforts to make a 44-hour prayer vigil on my behalf. That meant at the beginning of each hour some member would spend a few moments in prayer or sacrifice asking the Lord to bless me in a special way throughout the three-day experience.

A schedule was posted on the modern household's communication center—the refrigerator door—and the assigned person wrote in afterwards his or her endeavor.

For example: "Cleaned our room without being asked." "Wrote Father a letter." "Read from the Acts of the Apostles." "Served Mass and prayed for you." "Sent money to a family whose husband died." "Cleaned the turkey and offered it up for you." "Did the dishes." "Said a decade of the rosary for you."

During this round-the-clock vigil, the adults reserved the difficult night hours for themselves, setting an alarm, waking up, then praying or reading for several minutes.

Nevertheless, the very young also participated. A year-old child joined in the family prayer, too, and a first-grade girl "went to church and lit a candle with her own money," "made Father a card" and "gave up television all day and all night Sunday."

This type of prayer and fasting for others who are making a Marriage Encounter is not at all uncommon in the movement. In fact, Sunday morning throughout the United States (and soon, the leaders hope, the world) encountered couples consciously pray and sacrifice for persons experiencing at that very moment a particularly unique, challenging and profound aspect of the weekend.

Called the 90-90, it involves a lengthy writing and dialoguing period, often pivotal to the spouses' successful encounter. After this portion of the Marriage Encounter, each couple or priest is handed a sealed envelope. Inside a note tells you that someone agreed to be your "praying couple" for the weekend and has been remembering you before God throughout the three days. Aware from my contact with veteran Marriage Encounter personnel that this agreement to "pray for you" is not a mere formality, I was moved to tears when I read on my original weekend that the entire Fulton Marriage Encounter community had accepted this responsibility for me.

We also heard from the team leaders illustrations of impressive acts of prayer and sacrifice made by previously encountered couples on behalf of those experiencing the weekend. These included, for example, sleeping on the floor Friday and Saturday nights, abstinence from alcohol through the 44 hours, and no food on Sunday until noon.

Such instances of prayer and self-denial for others have always stirred up my own heart and fostered within me a strong desire (not always implemented, however) to do likewise. Still, following the original weekend, I found myself caught up more intensely than customary in this encounter spirit. When team couples known to me are presenting their weekends, I am surprised by the degree, ease and joy with which I both pray and sacrifice for them.

Several months later in talking about that aspect of Marriage Encounter to a young religious sister, I detected a puzzled, questioning look on her face. She was impressed by my obvious enthusiasm and the deeds done, but I judged this woman remained unconvinced about the notion and value of self-abnegation for others.

In her own life, this sister is extremely generous, hardworking and full of love for others. However, that uncertainty she felt about the worth of suffering, sometimes even self-imposed, for others left me now a bit confused.

Don't Lenten sacrifices made for another have value before God? Is it silly to offer for others the pain and distress experienced in a dentist's chair? Have Trappists performed in vain vicarious penances for those in need outside the monastery walls? Why did I give up the sports page for those weekends?

Her doubts, of course, made me rethink the question and in the process look at scripture as well as the Church's tradition. As a result, I am more convinced than ever that the Marriage Encounter practice stands squarely in the best of our Catholic Christian heritage, although how God views these sacrifices remains, naturally, a mystery to be grasped only later.

In Old Testament days Queen Esther and her Jewish people immediately turned to prayer and fasting when they faced unjust condemnation (the Book of Esther, Chapters 3-5).

A high-ranking official, Haman, angered by the Jewish leader Mordecai's refusal to kneel and bow down before him, gave an order supposedly in the king's name "that all the Jews young and old, including women and children, should be killed, destroyed, wiped out in one day. . ."

> When Mordecai learned all that was happening, he tore his garments, put on sackcloth and ashes, and walked through the city crying out loudly and bitterly, till he came before the royal gate, which no one clothed in sackcloth might enter. (Likewise in each of the provinces, wherever the king's legal enactment reached, the Jews went into deep mourning, with fasting, weeping, and lament; they all slept on sackcloth and ashes.)

Mordecai then communicated their plight to the queen, reminding the beautiful woman of her Jewish origin and asking Esther to intercede with the king.

Esther recalled for Mordecai the regulation by which anyone who appeared before the king without being summoned was subject to automatic penalty of death unless he extended the golden scepter and thus spared that person's life. Since she had not been so called for a month, Esther feared for her life. However, after further importuning by Mordecai, the queen responded:

> Go and assemble all the Jews who are in Susa; fast on my behalf, all of you, not eating or drinking, night or day, for three days. I and my maids will also fast in the same way. Thus prepared, I will go to the king, contrary to the law. If I perish, I perish!

Mordecai did as commanded and

> Queen Esther, seized with mortal anguish, likewise had recourse to the Lord. Taking off her splendid garments, she put on garments of distress and mourning. In place of her precious ointments she covered her head with dirt and ashes. She afflicted her body severely; all her festive adornments were put aside, and her hair was wholly disheveled.
>
> Then she prayed to the Lord, the God of Israel, saying; "My Lord, our King, you alone are God. Help me, who am alone and have no help but you, for I am taking my life in my hand. . . . Save us from the power of the wicked, and deliver me from my fear.
>
> On the third day, putting an end to her prayers, she took off her penitential garments and arranged herself in royal attire.

The king did in fact extend his golden scepter to Esther, learned of Haman's deceitful decree, freed the Jewish people and condemned that guilty leader to death on the gallows constructed originally for Mordecai.

Our Lord, both by his words and example, taught the value of prayer and fasting for others. As Savior, of course, he bore our sins in his body and delivered himself up for us. The cross itself became the perfect sign of a life given for others. Yet in many other ways and on different occasions he prayed or fasted or spoke of their value.

In the beginning of Jesus' public life as recorded in St. Matthew's Gospel, just prior to his call of Peter, Andrew, James and John, Christ was led into the desert by the Spirit where "he fasted forty days and forty nights, and afterwards was hungry" (Mt 4:1-2).

St. Luke tells us that our Lord "often retired to deserted places and prayed" (Lk 5:16).

Jesus frequently taught his listeners about the power of prayer. For example, "Ask, and you will receive. Seek, and you will find. Knock, and it will be opened to you. For the one who asks, receives. The one who seeks, finds. The one who knocks, enters" (Mt 7:7-8). Again, "You will receive all that you pray for, provided you have faith" (Mt 21:22).

That efficacy of prayer certainly must extend to our petitions for others.

Christ gives some directions about the way we fast, thus indirectly approving or encouraging the practice.

"When you fast, you are not to look glum as the hypocrites do. They change the appearance of their faces so that others may see they are fasting. I assure you, they are already repaid. When you fast, see to it that you groom your hair and wash your face. In that way no one can see you are fasting but your Father who is hidden; and your Father who sees what is hidden will repay you" (Mt 6:16-18).

Perhaps the best illustration of both Jesus' example and teaching about prayer and sacrifice for others occurs in regard to the healing of a possessed boy (Mt 17:14-21). A man brought to the Lord his son who was "demented and in a serious condition."

The father commented: "I have brought him to your disciples but they could not cure him."

Christ did at this very moment heal the troubled son. Later,

> The disciples approached Jesus at that point and asked him privately, "Why could we not expel it?" "Because you have so little trust," he told them. "I assure you, if you had faith the size of a mustard seed, you would be able to say to this mountain, 'Move from here to there,' and it would move. Nothing would be impossible for you. This kind does not leave but by prayer and fasting."

The history of the Church tells us of countless Christians, saints or otherwise, whose lives reflected a belief in those words, "this kind does not leave but by prayer and fasting." Many will recall, as an illustration, Pope John XXIII on his deathbed, offering those painful last moments for the welfare of others.

Even closer to our day, Donald Goergen in a book currently very popular among priests and religious, *The Sexual Celibate,* writes:

> Asceticism as self-imposed discipline or active self-purification is a constructive and necessary factor in spiritual growth—as constructive and necessary as self-discipline in any area of human life. . . . We can say only that such practices as abstinence, fasting, and meditation play a vital role in the Christian life. Spiritual direction or guidance and spiritual or religious counselling are also necessary. All these help the Christ in us come alive.[2]

---

[2] Goergen, Donald. *The Sexual Celibate.* New York: The Seabury Press, 1974, pp. 215-216.

On the Tuesday following one of those weekends conducted by a team couple from our area, the rectory phone rang and a brusque, strong, hurried male voice unknown to me said: "I want to talk to an encountered priest!"

He came to the rectory in a day or so and poured out the story of his religious conversion during that Marriage Encounter. The weekend achieved the usual marvels for him and his wife, but it also led this man to see he had been lying to himself for 25 years about the Church and God. Baptized and educated Roman Catholic, he had not participated in Mass over that quarter of a century except for his wedding ceremony. Even this religious event was arranged merely to please his devout parents.

An extremely bright, perceptive, professional individual, the man a few weeks later made his confession, received the Eucharist and resumed the practice of Sunday Mass abandoned so many years earlier.

After he left I felt a quiet, contented joy inside, as I remembered I had done my customary modest three days of prayer and fasting for those on that particular Marriage Encounter weekend.

13
Reaching Out

On Sunday mornings Angelo and Betty Miller with their three children participate in the 9:45 Mass at Holy Family. During Communion they approach the altar as a couple, receive the Eucharist, and then extend to the priest a small pouch with white cloth interior and soft plastic exterior.

Angelo holds the tiny purse in his hand while Betty unfolds a three-inch-square linen which had been tucked into a pocket of this receptacle. The priest then places a consecrated host upon the open cloth. Betty very carefully and reverently refolds the square material and places it in the pouch. Angelo inserts the purse in his coat and they return to their pew.

After Mass, the entire family climbs into their station wagon and travels 10 blocks to Jane Gray's house.

Jane retired from the nursing profession a decade or so ago. She owns the house, rents an upstairs apartment, has someone help with the cleaning, but rarely leaves the brown structure on the corner of Maple and West First Street. Most of her day is spent in a chair in the front room looking at passing traffic, watching television, talking with an ever-declining number of friends on the telephone, or reading the local paper. Once a month she has a regular visitor, the priest from Holy Family, who brings Jane Holy Communion and offers her the opportunity for the sacrament of Penance.

The woman's poor health makes it exceptionally difficult for her to navigate steps of the house as well as to climb into or out of a car. Trips around Fulton are fewer now. That confinement inside her pleasant home can prove quite lonely at times, she admits. This is particularly true since several of her bridge partners have died and hardly anyone is left with whom to play.

Jane will be waiting for the Millers. Waiting for the kiss from the husband and wife, for the hug from Kelly, Chuckie and little John, for the reading of that Sunday's scripture passages by Angelo and Betty, for the summary of the homily (sometimes the entire sermon has been tape-recorded), for the Eucharistic Lord Jesus they bring to her, for the recited prayers and blessings together, for the weekly bulletin from church, for the visit afterwards with this family.

Week after week Angelo and Betty follow this routine in fulfilling their function as ministers of Holy Communion to the sick. Through them Jane feels a greater sense of closeness to our Sunday worshiping community. She becomes a part of what is happening in the church so near and yet so far away. In addition, the always pleasant and patient woman now is able to receive Christ in the Eucharist weekly instead of only once a month as before when the priest came to call on her.

The Millers' concern for Jane Gray, however, reaches out beyond this weekly Sunday effort. Once they had been introduced to the woman and began their sacramental ministry to her, they found further big and little gestures of loving care to brighten her days: a mid-week visit from Betty, a telephone call from Angelo, a present from one of the children, a batch of cookies, a warm invitation to their home for the holiday.

Would the Millers have volunteered for this mission of mercy had they not made Marriage Encounter? It would be difficult to answer that question. There are equally generous and loving single persons and non-encountered couples who perform well the same task at Holy Family. Moreover, Angelo and Betty served the parish actively before their weekend.

Yet there seems a greater spark in their eyes now, a more eager willingness to build up the Church, a stronger desire to change the world. Certainly the decision to undertake this ministry as a couple and their joint decision for Angelo to enter the permanent diaconate received total support and much inspiration from Marriage Encounter.

The weekend tells a husband and wife in no uncertain terms they should become open and apostolic. You have great power, couple power, the team presenters stress, a power capable of building a new world somewhere.

Growing in closeness to each other by daily deepening their love for each other is seen as the essential and most potent method of making that dream a reality. Their unity as a couple will of itself speak to the world, to those they touch in daily life.

But simply loving each other will not alone change our society. The encountered husband and wife are encouraged to leave their weekend looking for ways to reach out, for avenues in which they as a couple particularly can contribute to the Church's growth. Those who present this Sunday afternoon exhortation, in typical Marriage Encounter fashion, do not leave their listeners with hopelessly astronomical ideals, totally bereft of any practical steps to achieve those goals. They list, one after another, pragmatic successfully tested procedures for broadcasting God's love for us and their love for each other.

Approaching the altar for Communion hand in hand as a couple is one. It tells, without doubt, the entire congregation the following Sunday that something *did* happen to the husband and wife on the previous weekend. However, not everyone rejoices over this display of marital closeness. Those uninformed about Marriage Encounter or opposed to it can and occasionally do object rather strongly to that practice.

At Holy Family we have found the use of couples as lectors a very positive development in our liturgies. It speaks silently, but also eloquently about "coupleness" and adds an effective variety to the presentation of God's word. Normally, one spouse proclaims the first reading, the other partner, the second. The petitions of the general intercessions or prayer of the faithful are divided between the husband and wife.

In at least one parish in the southern part of our diocese, couples (mostly encountered) have become the mainstays of the religious instruction program for junior high school teenagers. Moreover, this same approach has worked well with the youthful candidates for Confirmation. Such small group meetings at the couples' homes provide a warm setting, living examples of Christianity in practice, and a competent catechesis.

When one of our couples left Fulton for another state, during the first week or two in their new location they called at the rectory and invited the pastor for dinner. In the course of that evening meal, the husband and wife volunteered their services to him.

"We want to become involved in the parish, Father. Do you have any areas of particular need where we can assist?"

Their guest almost choked on his food. The Sunday before he had lectured parishioners about their apathy and the slowness with which they responded to necessary programs. In fact, he was struggling with personal discouragement because of that apparent indifference. The total willingness of this newly arrived encountered couple to accept any tasks presented them stunned the pastor.

A dozen couples at our parish form the core instructors for what we term a one-to-one, pre-Cana program. That technical title covers what has been a marvelously simple, intimate and highly successful procedure preparing engaged persons for marriage.

When a young man and woman come to the rectory for the arrangement of their wedding plans we give them three options to insure that they receive some premarital instruction. The young lovers may attend a diocesan-sponsored pre-Cana conference in a nearby city, participate in an engaged encounter weekend, or meet for an evening with one of our specially trained couples. About 75 percent select the third alternative.

Those dozen "instructors" had responded earlier to a bulletin invitation for assistance in this program. It was, of course, open to all couples of the parish, but only encountered partners in fact accepted the offer.

Their training consisted solely of a visit on my part with the first married couple, a printed list of 10 discussion topics distributed to the others, plus frantic telephone calls to the "experienced" teams from husbands and wives about to host their initial evening.

The list only cited subjects they should cover during the two-hour session, topics such as communication, finances, parents, love, sex, forgiveness. It did not provide either developmental material or an outline for the presentations.

At first the married couples were furious over this lack of training and nervous about the outcome. That changed immediately after the evening with an engaged couple. The results were almost universally positive with the fiances often quite enthusiastic.

Much of its success is due to Marriage Encounter. During and since their weekends these husbands and wives had dialogued at length about all 10 topics. Those deep exchanges gave them a facility in articulating profound observations, an ease in speaking about these matters more than they realized. In addition, and probably of greater significance, the Marriage Encounter insistence on each couple's specialness before God taught the encountered "instructors" to respect the engaged partners and not lecture or talk down to them.

Invariably, I heard the fiances remark: "We were nervous at first, but so were they. However, they made us feel at home and seemed really to care about our marriage. We just talked and at the end we thought they got as much out of the evening as we did."

Often the sessions continued until 11:00 or 11:30, far beyond the expected two-hour limit. Occasionally a close and ongoing relationship develops, with the married couple receiving an invitation to the wedding and a Christmas card months later.

In many ways this one-to-one premarriage program has become a perfect outlet for an encountered couple's apostolic zeal.

That reaching-out spirit also includes a reaching in, an effort to foster love among all members of the family. Marriage Encounter is not limited to the relationship between husband and wife.

Some parents have found a family dialogue helpful in this regard. Usually once a week the father, mother and children gather around a lighted candle, pray briefly and informally, then write their feelings on a genuine question. Afterwards these love letters are read and the sentiments expressed gently discussed.

This is how a couple in our parish described their initial family dialogue:

The most beautiful experience of the whole week, though, was Saturday night when we did our first family dialogue. One question was "How do you feel about Marriage Encounter and how do you feel about Mom and Dad going out so often because of it?" I can't explain the closeness we all felt that night. The kids had a lot of questions about Marriage Encounter, and we realized that they had been feeling pretty left out of things—Louise especially (seventh grade).

In my letter I explained to the kids that what Daddy and I were doing we felt was really worthwhile, but they were still the most important people in our lives. I could hardly get through that letter, and as I fought back the tears, I looked up to see Julie (first grade) crying, too. She saw what a hard time I was having trying to read that letter and she felt sorry for me. Pretty soon we were all crying and laughing and hugging each other.

We had started out with a prayer and so we ended with one too and then Bobby (age four) blew out our family candle.

Not since our weekend have I experienced such love or felt God so close to us. We are going to try to have a family dialogue once a week now as we have found a beautiful new way of communicating with our children.

Another vehicle employed by a few encountered spouses for reaching in to the other household members has been the Family Weekend Experience.

In this development, husband and wife plus all the children seven years or older spend 44 hours with perhaps two dozen other families following a pattern very similar to the basic Marriage Encounter. Presentations cover the I, We, We and God, We, God and the World phases of a weekend, but they are more succinct (about 5-10 minutes) and include a variety of audiovisuals to aid in conveying the message. Instead of dialogue through writing after the presentation, the family engages in different activities designed to communicate mutual attitudes and feelings to one another.

There is little socializing between families on this weekend, with the concentration on communication within each family itself. Like the initial Marriage Encounter, this experience also has a future goal in mind—to encourage and facilitate a weekly family hour of dialogue.

Couples come to Marriage Encounter for various reasons. For example, they may have been impressed by the joyfulness of some returning spouses or simply felt curious about this mysterious weekend or sensed that somehow it might improve their own marital relationship.

They leave, however, as visionaries. They have the desire to reach out and to build a better tomorrow.

14

Some Pitfalls

"Joe, I thought during your talk, if you mentioned Marriage Encounter one more time, I would scream."

The critic was a priest friend present for a three-hour lecture on the liturgy and parish life. I started to apologize for my excessive enthusiasm, but he stopped me:

"It wasn't that. Those were helpful things you mentioned and I know Marriage Encounter has some good points. But the way these people raped my parish makes it hard for me to even talk about it."

His bad experience surprised me. The man is an excellent, progressive pastor with parishioners involved in every kind of activity. If anything, I would have expected him to be strongly committed to Marriage Encounter, possibly even a team priest and surely aware of the movement's enormous potential for good.

Because we had no opportunity for further discussion, I never did learn or understand the fundamental cause behind that conflict.

The incident and his bitterly critical remark do, however, serve to remind encountered personnel that not everyone feels as warmly about Marriage Encounter as we do. It also should help us keep a proper perspective about the weekend and its aftermath.

I have seen such rich spiritual benefits from Marriage Encounter—radical conversions from lives of sin, an immense spirit of joy among couples, great acts of unselfishness—that I personally am convinced the Holy Spirit is present in a unique way in the movement.

But the weekend, the follow-up programs, the organizational structure, the leaders and followers, the various instructional guidelines—all these are indeed very human. They have not been divinely revealed and do not enjoy infallibility. Every aspect can change; the movement itself may eventually lose its power and go the way of other similar enthusiastic trends in the Church. Marriage Encounter is not for everyone, nor is it essential for anyone's salvation. Helpful for many, yes; but not required for all.

It might, then, be healthy to indicate some of the possible pitfalls, with the hope that our enthusiasm does not blind us to these hurtful holes along our paths.

An Elitist Attitude

I have not yet met a couple who had made a Marriage Encounter who consciously felt they were superior to their friends who hadn't made one. Ultimately, of course, that is a matter of intention and attitude for which God alone is judge.

Nevertheless, their enthusiasm can convey this impression. The desire to be with other encountered partners is most natural, as is the wish for others to share what has been so magnificent for them. However, I have seen that desire and wish inflict deep hurts, create rifts among friends and produce a certain withdrawal from the mainstream of parish life.

As time elapses, couples seem either to lose some of their intense zeal or to expand the breadth of their love. The latter enables them to recognize that Christian love reaches out to all persons. The former rather obviously eases for them the problem of elitism.

The very term "pre-encountered," occasionally employed, itself mirrors the elitist pitfall. It suggests a sense of "We are the lucky, initiated ones; you may one day join us." That differs from a genuine concern and prayerful hope that other couples may be disposed to make a weekend.

Hugging and Kissing

A huge throng of encountered couples descended some time ago upon St. Susanna's, the English-speaking parish in Rome staffed by American Paulists. They walked hand in hand to Communion and gave their usual embraces to each other at an information night which followed.

Many of the proper Roman parishioners were quite taken aback or put off by this external display of affection.

One man in our Holy Family parish who made and enjoyed a Marriage Encounter remarks to this day, "I just don't go for all the hugging and kissing. That's not me. I can't do it."

The talks on a weekend never indicated he had to hug and kiss other couples. There were words about the importance of nonverbal communication between husband and wife, plus a stress on the need we have for mutual support from other spouses in pursuing the vision of Marriage Encounter. However, the kind of embracing which develops quite naturally is never explicitly mentioned, certainly not proposed as a necessary procedure or even a noble deed.

It just happens.

I felt a strong desire to express my inner joy with that kind of embrace to the encountered couples during my homecoming party. Sometimes words simply cannot convey an interior feeling which two persons share. Through that hug and kiss I was trying to say: "The weekend moved me deeply. I am glad I went. Your love and prayers touched me. My happiness inside is intense, but I don't know how or can't seem to put this into words."

The couple's embrace in effect responds: "We understand. Your joy makes us happy. We love you."

For the person who has not made an Encounter or the naturally reserved individual, these external manifestations of affection can be awkward or even offensive. Some critical of such behavior may be led to speak about the excesses of Marriage Encounter; a few nasty commentators have gone so far as to allude to sordid relationships existing among the couples. I have never seen or heard verified the latter situation.

As should be evident from this book, that type of embracing among couples has no essential connection with the key teachings or major thrust of Marriage Encounter, although in many ways it grows rather naturally from the bond of love which develops.

Couples who have been encountered for a long period of time and are deeply committed to Marriage Encounter's expansion seem to restrain their enthusiasm in this regard lest those displays alienate others and keep them from eventually making a weekend.

Intensification of Highs and Lows

A weekend does seem to increase a person's sensitivity to the feelings of others and to deepen that individual's own emotional experiences. Highs often appear higher and lows, lower.

The days and weeks after Marriage Encounter are frequently filled with great joys. Ultimately, of course, a certain letdown occurs which may be the reason why some people judge their lows are much lower as a result of the weekend.

Personally, my own joys have been much deeper and more frequent, but I cannot say that the lows or depressed periods are longer or more painful.

Is this good or bad? My concept of the holy, spiritual, saintly person used to be of an individual always calm and inwardly recollected. That presumed we should strive through prayer and self-discipline to attain an emotional middle point, avoiding the very high and extreme lows.

I recall reading in the Liturgy of the Hours this year the advice of an early Christian writer who suggested that we pray for prudence and wisdom lest in success our hearts become too confident and in adversity, too discouraged. Such advice seems similar to, but not exactly identical with my pre-Marriage Encounter vision of holiness and integration.

Now I have some doubts about that ideal. Is it in fact a stoical goal? Am I merely projecting my Joe Cool, John Wayne image of how a priest should act and feel? Have we promoted a false spirituality which grows suspicious of emotions and of persons who appear to follow their feelings? The questions here remain unanswered.

The practical consequence of this phenomenon, however, means encountered persons should be aware of the tendency to experience "lows" more keenly and not let those intensified down moments influence their love decisions to reach out toward each other and others.

Moreover, they ought likewise to avoid a strained seeking for those "highs." We would all like to live on a perpetual plateau of up feelings; as pilgrims in this vale of tears, as couples pledged to love and cherish in sickness and health, in good times and in bad, they cannot expect such a future. To chase after such an illusion would be the epitome of escapism and a failure to embrace the cross of Christianity.

During early Marriage Encounter days some in fact unwittingly fell prey to this unrealistic search. They sought from the joy of a couple during a Sunday night welcome-home party fuel for rekindling the high they tasted on their own weekends.

Indiscriminate Open Sharing

The weekend involves only interchanges between husband and wife. As we have mentioned, it is not a sensitivity session, group therapy or some sort of crowd counseling. Except for one very minor revelation at the beginning (to which I still object), spouses never need discuss their personal lives or feelings with any other couple or couples on the weekend.

There is an opportunity at one point for the spouses to share voluntarily what the Marriage Encounter is or has meant for them. A few do. Moreover, on the team-training weekend there are extensive periods given over to, once again, volunteer openness with the others present. Both of these moments can prove exceptionally inspirational.

After a weekend, the couples are encouraged to participate in a variety of follow-up activities, e.g., monthly renewals, regular image groups, weekly regional sessions. All of these, totally optional, are designed to support encountered spouses in their quest for togetherness and to promote effective daily dialogues.

In some of these there is considerable open sharing of very personal feelings and concerns among participating couples. Those exchanges can be helpful and inspiring; they also are potentially devastating and hurtful. It is one thing for husband and wife to disclose difficult and intimate feelings with each other; it is quite a different matter for a group to reveal similar sentiments among themselves.

I regret to say that I have observed in some instances those negative results of indiscriminate open sharing.

Dialogue or Else

Nearly 20 years ago I officiated at the wedding of a fine young couple. After a dozen years of marriage and three children, the wife died under tragic circumstances. In time, the widower married again.

They made a Marriage Encounter several years later, benefited from the experience and began to dialogue daily. This continued for nearly a year, but they stopped the practice entirely because of disagreements over its obligatory character.

I have found daily scriptural dialogues and occasional dialogues with others most beneficial. I would highly recommend or encourage them to married couples and weekend graduates.

Nevertheless, in the aftermath stages of Marriage Encounter (not so much on the weekend itself), there seems to arise a sense that the dialogue fits into an either/or category. Either you dialogue each day or forget about the weekend. The dialogue becomes a matter of obligation, neglect of which borders on sinfulness.

Some couples feel guilty because after the disappearance of their first fervor they give up dialoguing or practice it infrequently or engage in the exchange only several days each week. Others, like the spouses above, argue over the very fact that they do or don't, should or shouldn't, may or must dialogue. Those disagreements and anxieties can lead them to abandon any attempt at dialogue and often to avoid all Marriage Encounter contacts.

It seems to me the dialogue should be proposed to married couples as a most useful tool and daily dialogue as an ideal, but without any implication that couples have an obligation in conscience to dialogue.

Dialogue is a very effective means of fostering marital closeness, but the Lord has not made it essential for a person's salvation.

Pressure-packed Recruitment

The weekend normally fills participants with enthusiasm and the talks which present an apostolic vision to the couples urge them to recruit new spouses for Marriage Encounter. This technique does harness that zeal and also motivates many friends or relatives to follow their example by signing up for a future weekend.

Occasionally, however, the recruiters lean quite heavily on possible candidates, won't take "no" for an answer, and can leave the unwilling couple resentful or feeling guilty.

On my team-training weekend, one husband observed that their recruitment would be by example only, not through high-pressure tactics. "I was deprived of the gift of a weekend for two years because someone pushed me too hard. I don't want to repeat that mistake. Marriage Encounter is a beautiful experience and we want to lead couples to it, not push the weekend upon them."

With the exception of emotionally troubled persons, I know of no couple who would not derive some joy and benefit from Marriage Encounter. But granted the human condition, not every husband and wife will choose to make the 44-hour experience. Encountered personnel need to accept that reality of life, respect the unique freedom of others, and restrain expressions of disappointment or anger at the rejection of their recruitment effort.

Marriage Encounter, like the daily dialogue, can be a positive factor in a couple's life, but is not essential or required for their membership in the Church or their entrance into heaven.

Secrecy

One cannot describe a personal experience. The other must taste it on his or her own. For that reason Marriage Encounter people hesitate to sketch details of the weekend for fear of misunderstanding. This reluctance has a sound basis, but the attempts at concealment occasionally backfire and lead others to grow supicious or hostile.

This book contains many of the principles behind Marriage Encounter and explains some of its techniques. However, the text in no way could replace a weekend and does not exhaust the richness of Marriage Encounter. Honest answering of questions posed beforehand likewise should have the same effect—the dissolution of anxieties without diminishing the impact of a weekend.

Narrow View of Life

The weekend urges couples, as we saw in the last chapter, to reach out and build a better world. An ever-deepening love between husband and wife is the first and most important step in that effort. However, encountered spouses sometimes forget the lessons taught at Marriage Encounter. They come to believe their mutual closeness alone will achieve the new society or they limit their activities solely to encounter functions.

Dropping out of previous parish commitments, concentrating only on their husband-wife relationship, ignoring the painful problems of contemporary society, closing themselves off from other people, showing no interest in the positive developments of today's world—all these trends indicate a couple missed the full meaning of the call for them to become open and apostolic.

Marriage Encounter should expand a couple's horizons, not narrow that vision of life.

One-Partner Enthusiasm

"I wish my parents never made Marriage Encounter. All they do now is fight. Mom wants to go to all those meetings and Dad doesn't."

I am not clear just how commonplace this pitfall may be among encountered couples. This is a real quotation and thus at least in the eyes of some children the problem does exist. Does one partner (in this case the husband) object strongly to post-weekend activities? Or does that same reluctant spouse merely go along to please the other?

No comment needs to be made on this point.

Everything Is Beautiful

One sometimes gets the impression from Marriage Encounter couples immediately after the weekend that the words from this song have become true in their lives. Moreover, not only has everything become beautiful, but easy as well.

The same mundane problems are present, the identical burdens and crosses remain, yet a new vision seems to permeate all these sharp briars of life and turn them into rosebuds.

In time—a few weeks for some, many months for others—that romantic stage (like the fun and rainbow phases of marriage, priesthood *et al.*) gradually disappears and a certain disillusionment descends upon the couple. They wonder if it was all a dream, a mirage. Were we truly that happy? Was the joy of living and the ease in coping, real?

Such disillusioning thoughts and feelings can cause some couples to give up on dialogue or retreat entirely from Marriage Encounter activities. Others seem to catch a second wind and enter into a joyful stage which tends to be less emotional and more profound. The beauty of the weekend very much remains in their memory and its ideals stand clearly before them. But they have come to understand that attainment of those goals will entail hard work and persistent effort. Few things worthwhile in life come easily.

Neglect of Basic Virtues

Marriage Encounter graduates are strong on caring, sharing and reaching out. In many ways they display this to a remarkable degree. But they sometimes and strangely fail with regard to some of the lesser, day-in, day-out Christian virtues.

Being disorganized and late, thus inconveniencing others is one. Acting aloof to those who have not made an Encounter is another. Slipping into petty jealousies and rivalries is a third. Mulling over minor misunderstandings is still another. Canonizing the purely human structures of Marriage Encounter is another. Exaggerating the Marriage "community" or "family" to the detriment of other existing natural (e.g., neighborhood) or supernatural (e.g., parish) communities, yet another.

*   *   *

Having finished this list of pitfalls, I would like now to remind my readers that there are 14 other chapters in *Alone No Longer,* all most supportive of Marriage Encounter. Even in the present critical section I began by stressing my conviction that "the Holy Spirit is present in a unique way in the movement."

St. Paul likewise believed the Spirit was uniquely present among the Christians of Galatia. But he also insisted they constantly test their activities and evaluate their lives to discern the presence or absence of the Holy Spirit.

My point is that you should live in accord with the spirit and you will not yield to the cravings of the flesh. The flesh lusts against the spirit and spirit against the flesh; the two are directly opposed . . . it is obvious what proceeds from the flesh: lewd conduct, impurity, licentiousness, idolatry, sorcery, hostilities, bickering, jealousy, outbursts of rage, selfish rivalries, dissensions, factions, envy, drunkenness, orgies and the like. I warn you, as I have warned you before: those who do such things will not inherit the Kingdom of God! (Gal 5: 16-17, 19-21).

I have experienced and suffered through some of those products of the flesh in Marriage Encounter.

In contrast, the fruit of the spirit is love, joy, peace, patient endurance, kindness, generosity, faith, mildness, and chastity. Against such there is no law! Those who belong to Christ Jesus have crucified their flesh with its passions and desires. Since we live by the spirit, let us follow the spirit's lead. Let us never be boastful, or challenging, or jealous toward one another (Gal 5: 22-26).

I have also tasted some of those fruits of the Spirit in Marriage Encounter. The next and concluding chapter will look at those positive effects of the movement.

15
Joy

The day before leaving Rome and returning home for the Christmas holidays I watched two students taste pure joy and heavy sorrow.

After our public morning prayer at 7:00, I ran into Mike, a tall, blond, bespectacled seminarian. His face was beaming with a smile and his eyes sparkled with joy.

"Mike, what makes you so happy at this ungodly hour of the morning?"

"I am on my way to the airport. My folks are coming in for an 18-day vacation."

Perhaps an hour or two later, I bumped into another student who asked:

"Father, when are you going home?"

"Tomorrow, Bill."

He then responded with some positive remarks like "that's great" or "have a good time" or "look forward to seeing you when you come back."

Those verbal statements of enthusiasm, however, clashed with what I saw in his eyes, his face, throughout his entire body. Bill's shoulders sagged with sadness;

his face forced a smile; the man's eyes betrayed deep sorrow and seemed to be looking far off in the distance.

Unlike Mike, Bill's parents would not be with him for Christmas. They will be at home, in New York, over 5,000 miles and nine hours away. My departure the next day for the United States simply made him more keenly aware that he would be separated at this season from those he loves the dearest and whose love for him is the strongest.

Those incidents illustrate rather well, I think, what St. Thomas Aquinas in his famous *Summa Theologica* taught about joy, sorrow and love.

Both joy and sorrow, he wrote, proceed from love, but in quite different ways. Joy is "caused by love" either because the person loved is present or the goodness of the one loved somehow exists within the other. Sorrow, on the other hand, "arises from love, either because the person loved is absent or is afflicted with some harm or is deprived of some goodness."[1]

Mike felt joy because his beloved parents would be with him for the holidays; Bill tasted sadness or sorrow because he would be separated from his father and mother.

Closeness to a person we love and who loves us brings joy. That delight, however, is not complete or total, since in this life the union does not last permanently and we can always grow closer to our beloved. The deepest and lasting joys are yet to come.

But real, true and deep joy we do experience.

Consider:

Parents finding their four-year-old child lost in the huge shopping mall of a strange city.

---

[1] Goergen, *op. cit.*, pp. 220-223.

The teenage girl being asked by a highly desirable young man to her first formal dance.

A woman in love receiving on Christmas Eve that surprise diamond.

The anxious lover hearing his beloved say, "yes."

Newlyweds discovering they will become parents.

A mother and father reading an apologetic love letter from their often rebellious and hurtful child.

Grandpa and grandma being hugged by adoring grandchildren.

The ultimate goal of Marriage Encounter is closeness between spouses, union of husband and wife, "the two of them become one body." For the priest that ideal means a similar closeness with Christ and his spouse, the Church, the people he serves. This closeness experienced on weekends and afterwards can and has produced intense joy for many, joys equivalent to those described above.

Therese and Harry are a couple in their late 50's or early 60's. Both suffered through painful first marriages. Harry's wife left him for another man; Therese's spouse was alcoholic, irresponsible and abusive—in time she left with her children to make a "new life for myself and them."

She and Harry did not meet until many years later and "even then I declined being too friendly with the man. Perhaps I felt he was the one for me, but I didn't even dream we could ever have a life together."

Nevertheless, their acquaintance, friendship and love grew and, finally, they did marry, although without a Catholic ceremony because of the previous marriages.

Her words below tell the story of their closeness and joy during and after the Marriage Encounter.

This is our love letter to you. Because of you and two of our very best friends we went on a weekend encounter. Despite the fact that my mom had a short-term illness which called us out to her side for about an hour and a half, we had the most beautiful weekend two people could ever have shared together.

Harry and I have been together for nine years, but before this weekend we were not as close as we thought.

We were truly married at our encounter weekend Mass. Twenty-four couples were our attendants. As we stood there together repeating the vows of marriage, we knew that good things were in store for us because God was there blessing us and our life together.

Ours, we feel, is even more special than the rest because ours is a true love one for the other. We live as brother and sister, but we don't mind because it isn't necessary for anything else to make us happy. We feel no need for anything else. God has accepted us as a couple. Because you understood and were forgiving toward us we now have a new and better life together.

We only wish we could reach out and encompass the whole world with our love. Since this is not possible we are trying to start, or keep going a chain that perhaps someday will touch the whole world.

Soon we are having our first information night. If we can, it is only the first of many. We want all the couples we know to enjoy a weekend like ours.

My Harry says that he didn't even realize how much he cared about me and my feelings or that sometimes he had failed by not taking these feelings into consideration. I, too, realized that part of my life was shut to him. We have promised each other that from now on we will share everything. Not just all the happy things, but sad ones, too. With emphasis on the latter ones, because I never shared the loss of my son with Harry. I kept it all to myself. This was wrong I know now and I am happier for finding this out. It was due to the encounter weekend also that I realized this fact.

We will work hard to spread this happiness to as many as we can reach and never stop trying to reach more.

I would like to share with you as I did with Harry one thought that I put in my love letter to him on our first night. I told Harry that I was so happy and excited about our weekend and our life together from now on that, if he turned the light out I would glow with happiness lighting up the whole room. This is truly how I feel about life now. Our life together before was a good one, but now we know how to make it better. We feel now that we do have God's blessing on our marriage. Perhaps someday we can have the Church's blessing, too.

Several months later, Therese wrote again:

We are doing well with our love letters and our dialogue each evening. It is bringing us closer and closer together in our unusual relationship. We are happier now than we have ever been.

Bill and Noreen took half of their eight children on a Family Weekend Experience.

The Sunday morning presentation centers around forgiveness or reconciliation. Each member of the family thinks of all the others and writes down one way in which he or she has in the past hurt every individual. Then, later, there are a series of quiet, private, one-to-one "forgiveness encounters."

Bill described with tears the pain and joy for him and for his oldest son as they admitted the hurt afflicted on each other and asked the other's pardon.

The love between husband and wife, parents and

children after a hurting, then apologizing, then forgiving incident is different, but deeper. With that deepening love comes a greater closeness and a more exquisite joy.

Sam and Janet, in their late 20's, have been teaching in the public schools since graduation from college. They have been married about a half dozen years, and they received a unique bundle of joy this fall. His letter gives the details.

Joyce and I have not started reading in church yet, but we have some wonderful news that we wanted to tell you. We have been trying to start a family now for a few years. We looked into adopting. Well, it's paid off. Last Wednesday we received a phone call and were asked if we were still interested in adopting. A baby boy was born the next day at 12:21 p.m. He was given up by his mother and he now lives with us. He is one week old today and in six months we can legally adopt.

Our life has really been falling into place since we have been attending the parish. We made a weekend after listening to your talk and now, a baby boy. God sure has shown his love for us.

Joyce is taking time off from school for now. She doesn't really want to go back because she would rather stay home with our son. I can't really blame her—he's a beautiful baby. We were supposed to bring him home Monday, but they wouldn't discharge him from the hospital until Tuesday. Monday morning was a big disappointment, but Tuesday was a beautiful day. We have prayed every night—first praying that he would be healthy and now praying to thank the Lord for all that he has done for us. My wife and I are riding on cloud 9.

In chapter 13 on "Reaching Out," I described one couple's initial experience with family dialogue and their reaction to it. A second letter some months later offers some additional insights into that exchange and presents a rather elegant testimony about the joys felt as a result.

It was so good to hear from you. You sound very happy and that makes us happy. Love is amazing, isn't it? No matter how many people we love, there is always room for more. What a joyous feeling it is whenever we think of you and your students working, caring and sharing together.

Our family dialogue continues to be a source of joy for all of us. It's funny. My husband and I were given so much on our weekend; our hearts were so full we never dreamed there could be more. Yet, God has given us still another gift, one just as beautiful as the first—our family dialogue. It feels like Christmas morning when you think you have opened all your gifts and then discover that there is one more hidden far back under the branches.

Joy sometimes comes in the midst of pain or after the resolution of a thorny issue. The joyful feeling I have tasted in such circumstances is more of a deep peace, a serenity or calmness, a strong, powerful current surging throughout my being. Like the service person who has completed boot camp or the graduate student who just finished his oral examinations, I usually feel I passed (normally not with a 100 percent mark, however) the test God has allowed to happen and made it through a crucible of fire somehow in the divine plan.

Two couples and I went through such a purifying death-rising, pain-joy experience.

We were involved in planning an exciting, challenging, potentially influential Marriage Encounter event. Just prior to our discussions a decision from above was made completely changing the outlook and approach. It crushed me and saddened them.

That evening we talked, prayed, discussed and worked through intense feelings of sorrow, pain, anger and resentment.

The next day we spent seven hours of hard-nosed study in preparation for the forthcoming project, despite our weariness and negative feelings.

By that night a peace spread over all of us. I felt it myself praying privately for a half hour in church. I could likewise see the strong serenity in their eyes afterwards as we wrapped up our deliberations and decided on the future of this program.

Whether we agreed or disagreed with the decision didn't seem so important to us now. For we believe the Father and the Holy Spirit are behind our lives and that somehow our anguish fits into the picture the Lord is working out for us. For some reason, God permitted this test, this trial. We felt a quiet, joyful calm, like a still sea at sunset, after having worked through that two-day struggle.

St. Paul once wrote to the Christian community at Colossae:

> Even now I find my joy in the suffering I endure for you. In my own flesh I fill up what is lacking in the sufferings of Christ for the sake of his body, the church. . . For this I work and struggle, impelled by that energy of his which is so powerful a force within me (Col 1:24; 29).

My Sunday departure from Holy Family for Rome was a deeply emotional experience.

The farewell applause at the end of Mass brought tears streaming down my face. Thanks to Marriage Encounter, I didn't seek to conceal or struggle to hold back those tears.

The final embraces at the Syracuse airport meant more of the same.

When I walked onto the Alleghany jet, my cheeks were damp and eyes red. Two women who had observed the waiting area scene smiled and said, "Your parishioners really love you, don't they?"

Finally seated and cramped in between two other passengers, I waved through the window a last good-by and then opened up two letters handed me just prior to boarding the plane. Those notes repeated in writing the loving support offered in other ways at the terminal gate.

The woman next to me, as she observed my moistened cheeks and emotional distress, must have thought I had been defrocked, or at least exiled to some foreign land.

All the tears, all the weeping, however, were more tears and weeping of joy than of sorrow. Pobably a quarter of the emotion was a sadness in leaving these beloved people of the parish. The main thrust, on the other hand, of that experience was an overwhelming joy, an inexpressible good feeling caused by the sense of being genuinely loved.

Epilogue:
The Same Old Me?

Normally after a retreat I feel a dramatic letdown. During those days of prayer, conferences, quiet and reflection, I would always rekindle past ideals, make very practical resolutions, and redirect the movement of my life towards a more fruitful future. However, almost as soon as I walked through the rectory door afterwards, the world outside the retreat house rudely and roughly hit me in the face.

Usually, something had gone wrong in the parish and the consequent immediate termination of that idealistic and spiritualized atmosphere made me edgy and irritable. Reentry into the real world was painful and disillusioning. I had to face and accept the same old me.

Typically, I returned from my 44-hour weekend riding on cloud nine. But this time my feelings were not the elation brought on by a magnificent spring morning or the joy of a victory or honor. Instead, I experienced a profound peace and serenity, an inner stillness and clarity which lasted through very contrary situations and troublesome events.

For example, I walked to the rectory drained, but deeply happy after my tear-filled welcome-home party.

The house was dark and silent, except for the steady ping of raindrops hitting a dozen pots and pans scattered around the second-floor hallway. These makeshift buckets more or less satisfactorily caught the water coming through the ceiling, but apparently neither our house-keeper nor my priest-partner had thought to check its source—the attic above. For the next two hours I bumped around the attic with matches, flashlight and pails seeking to capture the gallons of water streaming down through the roof.

On Tuesday of that week one of our young parish-ioners died in an industrial accident. He had been married just over a year, and his first child had been baptized the week before.

Thursday I missed a plane connection in New York through the error of a priest who had hosted me for some conferences. His oversight caused me considerable hardship and uncertainties after an already fatiguing day.

But despite the sort of difficulties which can place severe demands on our patience, test our resources and frequently rob us of personal peace, my post-Marriage-Encounter serenity and joy survived. Now, nearly a year after my basic weekend, the question arises: is it the same old or a brand-new me?

From the distance provided by a year's testing, I'm convinced that a positive transformation has occurred. The old me has become a better, a happier, a more effec-tive person.

Throughout these chapters, I have tried to illus-trate the more significant changes I experienced be-cause of the weekend. Today I continue to observe some very definite and measurable shifts in my behavior. My time spent in prayer has doubled, my ability to exercise self-discipline has increased, my awareness of the needs of the people around me and my capacity to respond to those needs has begun to develop. On a deeper, more interior and thus less observable level, I feel an enormous change in my attitudes, in my feelings.

But is all this growth an illusion? Do I sense a new me inside while others see the same old me on the outside? This I cannot answer. But I am certain that Marriage Encounter supplied me with a vision and an awareness of what I can and should become. It also gave me a taste of the joy which comes from loving and being loved. My responsibility now is to keep that vision and awareness before me and live them out day after day.

I no longer need to feel alone.